Worship in the

New Testament

by
C. F. D. Moule
Lady Margaret's Professor Emeritus in the University of Cambridge

GROVE BOOKS

BRAMCOTE   NOTTS.   NG9 3DS

CONTENTS

Copyright C. F. D. Moule 1961 and 1977

ABBREVIATIONS

B.J.R.L.	Bulletin of the John Rylands Library at Manchester
E.T.	Expository Times
H.T.R.	Harvard Theological Review
I.C.C.	International Critical Commentary
I.G.	Inscriptiones Graecae (1873 ff.)
J.B.L.	Journal of Biblical Literature
J.N.T.S.	Journal called New Testament Studies
J.T.S.	Journal of Theological Studies
R.B.	Review biblique
S.-B.	H. L. Strack and P. Billerbeck, Kommentar zum Neuen Testament aus Talmud and Midrasch (1922-8)
S.J.T.	Scottish Journal of Theology
T.W.N.T.	Theologisches Wörterbuch zum Nueen Testament (ed. G. Kittel and G. Friedrich, 1933-)
Z.N.T.W.	Zeitschrift fur die neutestamentliche Wissenschaft

ACKNOWLEDGMENT

The original book *Worship in the New Testament* was first published by the Lutterworth Press in 1961 in the series of 'Ecumenical Studies in Worship', and was reprinted in 1962 and 1964. It has long been out of print, and is now reproduced, by the kindness of the Lutterworth Press, from the original pages.

AUTHOR'S NOTE

I am grateful to Grove Books for inviting me to have this book reprinted. Ideally, this should have been the opportunity for extensive re-writing in the light of criticisms, and for bringing the bibliography up to date. But, as it has been impossible to undertake this, it has seemed better to reprint it exactly as it stood in 1961, apart from the correction of a few mistakes and the addition of a few references. As in 1961, I wish to express my thanks to Professor J. G. Davies, the Reverend A. R. George, and the late Professor E. C. Ratcliff, for their help and suggestions to me when I was writing the book.

C.F.D.M.

First Impression (this edition only—in two parts) December 1977 and March 1978

Reprinted (in one volume) August 1983

ISSN 0306-0608

ISBN 0 907536 52 2

H 3750

that he is a λειτουργός of Christ Jesus for the Gentiles, doing the priestly service of the gospel (ἱερουργοῦντα τὸ εὐαγγέλιον[1]), in order that the offering (προσφορά) of the Gentiles may be acceptable (εὐπρόσδεκτος), sanctified by the Holy Spirit (Rom. 15: 15 f.). To the Philippians he writes that he rejoices, even if he is to be poured out like a libation (σπένδομαι) over the sacrifice and service (θυσία καὶ λειτουργία) of their faith (Phil. 2: 17); and the same libation metaphor recurs in 2 Tim. 4: 6. But these terms are not reserved only for the great sacrifices of an apostolic life of evangelism. In the same letter to Philippi, not only is the Philippians' service to Paul described (2: 30) as λειτουργία (which, as we have seen, is not yet exclusively a technical term of worship), but also their gift of money is called an acceptable sacrifice, well-pleasing to God (4: 18)—a deliberately cultic phrase. These cultic metaphors, applied by Paul alike to his own ministry and to the service of others, are only a particularizing of the general description in Rom. 12: 1 of Christian self-consecration as the offering of our bodies as a living sacrifice, dedicated to God and acceptable to Him, which is our "logical" service (λογικὴ λατρεία), that is, a sacrifice on the level not of material gifts and animal sacrifices but of human reason and of all that is supra-material (cf. λογικὸν γάλα, 1 Pet. 2: 2): a sentiment expressed also in Heb. 13: 15 f., already discussed, and in 1 Pet. 2: 5 ff., in terms of spiritual sacrifice (πνευματικαὶ θυσίαι) offered in a spiritual temple (οἶκος πνευματικός) by people of God who are a holy and a royal priesthood (ἱεράτευμα ἅγιον, βασίλειον). Similarly, the persecuted, dispossessed, despised Christians of the Apocalypse have all been made "royal" and "priestly" by the death of Christ (Rev. 1: 6).

All Christian life is worship, "liturgy" means service, all believers share Christ's priesthood, and the whole Christian Church is the house of God (1 Cor. 3: 16; Eph. 2: 22).

Accordingly, on the Christian showing, worship cannot possibly be an optional extra. It is the business of life. If "there is no longer any 'cultus' in the ancient sense", it is equally true, conversely, that all life has become "cultus" in a new sense. Life has no other purpose than to be rendered up to God in adoration and gratitude. "Whatever you are doing", wrote St. Paul in Col. 3: 17, "in word or in deed, do all in the name of the Lord Jesus, giving thanks to God the Father through him". The true end of man is "to glorify God and enjoy him for

---

[1] Cf. 4 Macc. 7: 8 (v. l.).

ever".[1] The seer's way of describing the business of heaven is to let us hear the sound of multitudes of harpers harping on their harps and the rush of "Alleluias!" and the four creatures crying "Holy, holy, holy", and to let us see the Throne surrounded by rank on rank of prostrate worshippers. In our more literalist and prosaic moods this sounds monotonous. As the Devil says in *The Brothers Karamazov*, "Everything would be transformed into a religious service: it would be holy, but a little dull". But this is because we cannot yet live life whole nor have we the language to match real living. At present we are compelled to let work and worship alternate. Our work and recreation would be less efficient and worthy if we tried consciously to think of God while working out a mathematical problem or shooting a goal. But they would be selfish and secular if we did not at definite times give articulate expression to our whole life's dedication. It was perhaps both loss and gain that the New Testament Church had no buildings, as we have, dedicated expressly to worship. But it would undoubtedly have been all loss if they had not set apart special times to meet together at an agreed place for conscious worship.

But specialization is only a concession to human limitations. Ultimately, life has no meaning at all unless it is all for God and unless its whole aim is worship. That is why worship, in the more limited, specialized sense, becomes, in its turn, meaningless and barren unless it issues in life and work. In short, the New Testament vocabulary, and the attitude which it represents, point clearly enough to the conclusion that, beyond the limits of this world, worship and work are one and indistinguishable. Hence, as we enter a place of worship, we pray: "Go thou with us, O Lord, as we enter into thy holy house; and go thou with us as we return to take up the common duties of life. In worship and in work alike let us know thy presence near us; till work itself be worship, and our every thought be to thy praise; through Jesus Christ our Saviour."[2]

---

[1] From the Shorter Catechism of the Westminster Assembly, 1647.

[2] E. Milner-White and G. W. Briggs, *Daily Prayer*, 1941, 110. By permission of the Oxford University Press.

PROLOGUE

A DISTINGUISHED DUTCH scholar has spoken of "a certain 'pan-liturgism' which sees everywhere in the Pauline epistles the background of the liturgy whenever a simple parallel in wording between them and the *much later* liturgies is found";[1] and it is certainly true that it is fashionable at present for students of the New Testament to find liturgy everywhere. This is partly the result of a healthy swing of the pendulum away from a narrowly literary approach to the New Testament towards a vivid recognition that here are not "bookish" writings so much as the deposit of community life—and, in particular, the life of worshipping communities. Partly, also, it is due to the liturgical movement, with its reawakened concern for the theology and practice of worship in our own day.

Enthusiastically as these tendencies and movements are to be welcomed, they have brought with them the temptation to detect the reverberations of liturgy in the New Testament even where no liturgical note was originally struck. Granted that it is impossible to over-emphasize the importance of worship in any Christian community, ancient or modern, yet it is possible, in one's enthusiasm, to squeeze the evidence beyond its capacity.

An attempt is made, therefore, within the limits of this small book, to provide a sober presentation of the evidence for Christian corporate worship—for no attempt is made to pursue the big subject of individual, private worship—within the New Testament period. It is too much to hope either that such conclusions as are reached will command the assent of all, or that the frequent failure to reach positive conclusions at all will win the approval of many. But the aims of this book are limited, and they will have been achieved if in it the data for a reconstruction of Christian practice in the early days and of the motives behind it have been adequately displayed. And if the writer fails to detect "liturgy" in the more specialized sense everywhere, it remains true—and this is the most significant single fact for the student of liturgical origins—that the Christians of this period saw the worship of God as the whole purpose of life. They did not worship efficiency or security, regarding divine service on Sunday as a means to such ends: the meaning and end of all life was nothing other than the worship of God. An attempt is made in the epilogue to bring this out.

[1] W. C. van Unnik, "Dominus Vobiscum", in *New Testament Essays (in mem.* T. W. Manson, ed. A. J. B. Higgins, 1959), 272.

I

THE ROCK WHENCE YE WERE HEWN

DISTINCTIVELY CHRISTIAN WORSHIP bears the same sort of relation to Jewish worship as the distinctively Christian writings do to the Jewish scriptures. It was in the context of the use of the Jewish scriptures that the Christian traditions about the triumph and victory of God in Jesus Christ were first shaped and formulated and then written down. But they were not simply a parallel growth to Jewish scripture or a mere addition to it: the relationship was one at once of more intimacy and of greater contrast than that.

The starting-point of Christian tradition was what God had done in Christ. And since Christ was recognized by the Christians as having both fulfilled God's design and transcended the sketch of that design in scripture, the Christians found themselves both using and transcending the Old Testament scriptures. Moreover, since Christ was both recalled as a historical figure of the past, and also experienced as a contemporary presence in the Christian congregation, the authority of His remembered teaching merged with that of His inspiration still speaking through the lips of Christian prophets and men and women of God. Jesus was not only like a Rabbi of the past: He still continued to speak through His own interpreters.

Thus, on a foundation of Old Testament words, there arose a structure of teaching and incident recalled from the past, and of inspired contemporary utterance, to form a distinctive edifice, at once continuous, and yet also in striking contrast, with its Jewish antecedents.[1] The Christian scriptures are an organic union of Jewish scripture, Christian tradition, and inspired interpretation.

In the same way, Christian worship, like Christian literature, was continuous with, and yet in marked contrast to, Jewish worship. Like the Christian scriptures, it grew out of words borrowed, out of traditions remembered, and out of inspired utterances; and, as with the

[1] See O. Cullmann in *S.J.T.* III, 1950, 180 ff.; C. H. Dodd, *According to the Scriptures*, 1952; J. W. Doeve, *Jewish Hermeneutics in the Synoptic Gospels and Acts*, n.d., about 1953.

scriptures, so in worship, the Jesus who was remembered was found to be the same Jesus who was experienced and who was present wherever two or three were assembled in His name. Christian worship was continuous with Jewish worship and yet, even from the first, distinctive.

It is therefore with the Jewish "matrix" that we have to begin, for the sake both of comparison and contrast.[1] As is well known, the Temple at Jerusalem continued, until its destruction in A.D. 70, to be the focus of Jewish worship. The Jewish synagogue (an institution of obscure origin, but perhaps dating virtually from the time of the exile) was in essence simply a "gathering together" (which is what the Greek, συναγωγή, means) of a local group to hear the scriptures read aloud, to praise God and pray to Him together, and to be instructed. In theory at any rate, the synagogue system was not an alternative to the Temple cultus. Religion on the level of its national consciousness and in its official form still found expression in the sacrificial cultus at the single Temple, the one centre of world Judaism.

Indeed even when a worshipper was not himself offering a sacrifice, his prayers seem often to have been offered actually in the Temple, or at least linked with the hours at which sacrifice was offered. In Luke 1: 10 the whole congregation pray in the court while Zacharias offers the incense in the Holy Place (cf. Rev. 8: 3 f.); in Acts 3: 1 Peter and John go up to the Temple at the hour of prayer which was also the hour of the evening sacrifice (see Exod. 29: 39, etc.); and in Acts 10: 30 a God-fearing Gentile prays at the same evening hour. So in the Old Testament, in 1 Kings 18: 36 Elijah's prayer and offering on Mount Carmel are at the time of the offering of the oblation (cf. Ezra 9: 5); and in Dan. 6: 10 Daniel prays towards Jerusalem three times a day (cf. Ps. 55: 17). (Incidentally one may ask whether it is significant for the provenance of the traditions behind Matthew and Luke respectively that in Matt. 6: 5 ostentatious prayer is in the synagogue, but in Luke 18: 10 in the Temple. In Matt. 5: 23f., however, there is no doubt about the Temple being in view.)

"In theory," then, the synagogue was secondary to the Temple. But it has to be admitted that "in whose theory?" would be a legitimate question. For it is probably a mistake to imagine that there was any one

<hr>

[1] See C. W. Dugmore, *The Influence of the Synagogue upon the Divine Office*, 1944; O. S. Rankin, "The Extent of the Influence of the Synagogue Service upon Christian Worship", *The Journal of Jewish Studies* 1, 1948, 27 ff. (stressing the contrast).

Jewish "orthodoxy" in the New Testament period. Rather, we have to imagine various types of thought and practice existing side by side. No doubt the priestly aristocracy, mainly Sadducean, maintained that the Temple cult was essential, and alone essential. But equally, we have some idea, through the accounts of the Essenes in Philo and Josephus, and, recently, through the Qumran writings, of how differently a sectarian, but still priestly, group might be behaving at the same time.[1] Evidently the Qumran sect maintained a priesthood and a ritual organization, but one which was independent and sharply critical of the Temple hierarchy. Although not in principle opposed to animal sacrifice as such, they seem to have regarded the Jerusalem hierarchy as so corrupt that they must for the time being dissociate themselves from the system; and in the meantime, making a virtue of necessity, they were able to console themselves with the reflection that praise and prayer, "the offering of the lips", was equal in value to the traditional sacrifice.[2] In addition to groups which held such an attitude, it is just possible that there were extreme movements within Judaism which were opposed to the Temple cultus on principle, and were content with a synagogue type of worship alone—a kind of "Quaker" Judaism. Dr. Marcel Simon has published interesting speculations about this in connexion with the Christian martyr Stephen and the so-called "Hellenists" of Acts[3]; and it is possibly relevant to note that no lamb is mentioned in the accounts of the Last Supper itself (as distinct from its preparation, Mark 14: 12 and parallels). It is possible that this is only because the accounts of the Last Supper are influenced by later eucharistic practice; or it might be because the meal was no Passover; or, again, it might be (as Dr. Ethelbert Stauffer has suggested)[4] because

[1] Philo, *prob.* 75; Josephus, *Ant.* 18.1.5. The most important of the Qumran documents for this purpose is the so-called *Manual of Discipline* (designated 1 QS in current notation), which may be conveniently read in the annotated translation by W. H. Brownlee in *Bulletin of the American Schools of Oriental Research, Supplementary Studies,* nos. 10–12, 1951.

[2] See J. M. Baumgarten, "Sacrifice and Worship among the Jewish Sectarians of the Dead Sea (Qumran) Scrolls", *H.T.R.* XLVI, 1953, 154–7; J. Carmignac, "L'utilité ou l'inutilité des sacrifices sanglants dans la 'Règle de la Communauté' de Qumran", *R. B.* LXIII, 1956, 524–32.

[3] M. Simon, *St. Stephen and the Hellenists,* 1958, and earlier studies there cited. (I do not by any means agree with all his conclusions.)

[4] E.g. in *Jesus, Gestalt und Geschichte,* 1957, 86, Eng. trans. *Jesus and His Story,* 1960. B. Gärtner, "John 6 and the Jewish Passover", in *Coniectanea Neotestamentica* XVII, 1959, 46 ff., suggests that Jesus might the more easily have held a lambless but Passover-like meal on the day before the Passover if Jews of the

Jesus had already been banned as a false teacher by the officials of Judaism, and a heretic was not permitted a lamb. But might it, alternatively, be that Jesus was a non-sacrificing Jew? Or may it even be that Jesus, prescient in His anticipation of the fall of Jerusalem and the de-judaizing of the Gospel, deliberately attached His teaching not to the lamb (whether there was lamb on the table or not) but to those elements of the food and drink which would always be available?

But that was a digression about varieties of attitude within Judaism. The important point for the present purpose is that the Christian Church was born within a context of Temple and synagogue; indeed, it has always been tempting to find already there the two components of Christian worship—the Sacraments, corresponding to the Temple, and "the Word", corresponding to the non-sacrificial, non-sacramental synagogue, with its strong element of reading and instruction. Accordingly, there have been times when what is now represented in the Anglican Church by Matins and Evensong and by the "Ante-Communion" has been traced to the synagogue service, while "the Liturgy", the Holy Communion or Eucharist proper, has been treated as a kind of counterpart to the sacrificial and the cultic in Judaism.

But in fact neither Judaism nor Christianity is so simple as to be fairly stylized in this manner; and it will be better simply to note the Jewish setting and to see what picture of Christian worship emerges from such evidence as we possess, before we try to make rash generalizations or formulate principles. While we are thinking, however, about the various components of worship, it is perhaps worth while to remark in passing that the whole history of worship might be written round the fascinating and difficult question of the relation between the outward and the inward; and that something is undoubtedly lost (whatever corresponding gains there may be) when such external expressions as, let us say, corporate movement form no part of worship. Whether for Judaism or for Christianity, the absence of scope for rhythmic movement, for choral chanting, for the throwing of the whole body into the expression of worship, is going to make a considerable difference—perhaps both for better and for worse—in the whole manner of

dispersion were familiar with such celebrations when they could not come up to Jerusalem. Evidence that this was the case is scanty, but he cites Josephus *Ant.* 14.10.8 for Jews in Delos, and Mishnaic evidence for the usage in Palestine outside Jerusalem. So M. Black, "The Arrest and Trial of Jesus" in *New Testament Essays* (as in Note 1, p. 3), 32 refers to "the [Passover] celebrations in the synagogue, especially in the Diaspora, without a paschal lamb." See further A. Jaubert, "Jésus et le calendrier de Qumran", *J.N.T.S.* VII, 1, October 1960, 23.

worship.[1] The same applies—again, both positively and negatively—to the wearing of special garments, and to colour and ornament generally.

Whatever may have been the circumstances in which the Apocalypse was written, the scenery of heaven which it presents—with the ceremonial dress, the loud noise, the rhythmic movement, and the ordered arrangement—seems to reflect an appreciation of the place of these things in worship. It might even represent a "compensation", in vision, for one who, by his faith, as well as (perhaps) by the fall of the Temple, had become cut off from the stately splendour of worship at Jerusalem.

But of course there is gain as well as loss in being driven to an almost static simplicity; and the ideal is probably only reached when the two can be combined. Little "cells" of friends worshipping informally but also converging periodically for the more formal public worship; the alternation of the "Quaker" and the "Catholic" emphasis, of the inward and the outward—it is by such means that the whole person is most likely to be drawn up into a total attitude of worship.

If, now, we attempt a reconstruction of the manner of worship in the early Church, the Acts will provide an important field of inquiry. But before looking at this evidence, it is right to ask what may be discovered about Jesus' own attitude during His ministry.

It is impossible to doubt that He worshipped in the Temple. All four Gospels preserve allusions to this. According to Luke, He is found in the Temple as an infant when His parents bring Him to be presented as their first male child, in accordance with the Law; and again when He goes up to Jerusalem as a boy for His first Passover. According to the unanimous witness of all four Gospels, it was when He had come to Jerusalem for the Passover that He was arrested and put to death. The Fourth Gospel expressly mentions His presence in the Temple also for the "feast of tabernacles" (John 7: 2 f.) and for the winter festival of *Hannukkah* or Dedication (John 10: 22).

What is not expressly evidenced is that Jesus Himself ever offered an animal sacrifice. The nearest that the Gospels come to it is in sayings which might suggest approval of the sacrificial system (Mark 1: 44 and parallels and Matt. 5: 23 f.). But such sayings can hardly be pressed to mean positive approval of sacrifice. The meaning of Matt. 5: 23 f. is, in fact, almost identical with that of Christ's quotation from Hosea, "I desire mercy and not sacrifice" (Matt. 9: 13; 12: 7); and although that only means that mercy is more important than sacrifice, one cannot

[1] See the reference to *movement* in the worship of the Therapeutae in Philo, *vit. cont.* 84 (cited by G. Delling, *Der Gottesdienst im Neuen estament*, 1952).

help wondering whether (as has already been suggested) Jesus Himself possibly worshipped without sacrificing. Further attention must be directed to this in connexion with the Last Supper.

However, that Jesus cared about the Temple worship, whether or not He actually joined in sacrifice, is evident enough, if only from the story of the expulsion of the dealers from its outer court. Whether this was an attack upon mercenary-mindedness or a gesture towards the Gentiles, in either case it betokens a reckless zeal for the reform of the Temple. It is difficult to see it as an attack upon the Temple system as such.

Equally clearly, however, Jesus also saw that the Temple was doomed. The charge that He had said "I will destroy this Temple . . ." was not, according to Mark 14: 57-59, substantiated. But that He had indeed said something that might have been so interpreted, emerges from the taunts levelled at Him in Mark 15: 29 (parallel to Matt. 27: 40). And in the introduction to the apocalyptic discourse (Mark 13: 2 and parallels) He foretells the destruction of the Temple; while John 2: 19 has the saying "Destroy this temple and in three days I will raise it"; and Matt. 12: 6, "something greater than the Temple is here". There is enough in these traditions to explain the attitude of Stephen (Acts 6: 14) who is accused of saying that Jesus is going to destroy "this place".

If there is no doubt that, despite these reservations, Jesus worshipped in the Temple, it is equally clear that He regularly went to synagogue on the sabbath (cf. Acts 17: 2, of Paul). In Luke 4: 16 it is expressly described as His custom to do so; and even if we were to discount this as evidence, there is, all over the Gospels, a sufficient number of references to Jesus teaching and healing in synagogues to leave us in no doubt on this score.

It is sometimes alleged that in synagogue Jesus would necessarily have recited the entire Psalter in the course of public worship. Of this there is no clear evidence. That the Psalter was at some period divided into sections corresponding with the lectionary cycles for other parts of the scriptures[1] neither proves that this held good for the time of Christ nor that, even if it did, all the Psalms in the sections were publicly used. This is worth mentioning, since the indiscriminate use in certain branches of Christian worship of the entire Psalter, including the fiercely nationalist and bloodthirsty songs, is sometimes defended on

---

[1] See A. Guilding, "Some Obscured Rubrics and Lectionary Allusions in the Psalter", *J.T.S.n.s.* III, 1, April 1952, 41 ff., and *The Fourth Gospel and Jewish Worship*, 1960.

the ground that Jesus Himself used them all. One can only ask "Did He?" and, even if He did, would that necessarily be determinative (any more than the use, if that were substantiated, of animal sacrifices) for the post-resurrection practice of the Christian Church?

That Jesus was steeped in the scriptures, including the Psalter, is suggested by the sayings attributed to Him in the Gospels. But the same evidence seems to suggest also a very considerable freedom in selection.

In sum, then, it may be said that, while Jesus used at least some of the Jewish institutions of worship, and apparently did so with ardour and great devotion, He refused to shut His eyes to the nemesis which was to overtake a Temple which had been made mercenary and exclusive; He saw in His ministry and in His own self the focal point of the "new Temple"; and He was satisfied with nothing but the absolute sincerity and spirituality of which the Temple was meant, but too often failed, to be the medium: "the hour cometh and now is when neither on this mountain [at Samaria] nor in Jerusalem shall they worship the Father . . . the true worshippers shall worship the Father in spirit and in truth" (John 4: 21, 23).

The practice of private prayer by Jesus is too familiar a matter to require more than mention here,[1] and, in any case, private prayer is not the subject of this inquiry; but the immensely significant address *Abba* which Jesus used in His own prayer to God will be discussed at a later point.

Coming now to the Acts, we find at once that the apostles in Jerusalem seem, as a matter of course, to have gone to prayer, at first, at any rate, in the Temple. We have already noticed the reference (Acts 3: 1; cf. Luke 18: 10; 24: 53; Acts 2: 46) to Peter and John going there; and there are references to Paul not only worshipping in the Temple (Acts 22: 17) but being ready to pay the expenses of sacrifice for a group of men, presumably poor men, as an act of Jewish piety (Acts 21: 23–26). In the same way, contact is scrupulously maintained with the synagogue by such as Stephen (Acts 6: 9) and Paul (Acts *passim*), both in Jerusalem and outside Judaea in the dispersion, until they are expelled from it. Expulsion from the synagogue inevitably took place sooner or later (as John 16: 2, cf. 9: 22, implies, and Acts 18: 6 f. bears witness); and it is likely that the final recognition that

[1] There is a valuable section on this in A. R. George, *Communion with God*, 1953. See also K. H. Rengstorf's Commentary on Luke (*Das Neue Testament Deutsch*, 1958), 251-3.

Christianity was incompatible with non-Christian Judaism had far-reaching influence on the shaping of Christian ways of worship.

But that was not immediately; and in the meantime not only were the Jewish places of worship retained by the Christian Jews but doubtless also the Jewish religious calendar. Many, at least, of the early Christians are to be assumed to have gone on observing the sabbath (Saturday) even if the next day of the week (Sunday) eventually came to occupy a dominant position as the day of the resurrection (Ignatius *Magn.* 9: 1, Barnabas 15: 9, etc.; cf. Rev. 1: 10 and the vision which follows). In any case, the sabbath (Saturday) remained in Jewish societies the only day free for worship (in Gentile societies there was no *weekly* free day, only the pagan festivals at irregular intervals); and it is likely enough, as H. Riesenfeld suggests,[1] that the Christians began simply by prolonging the sabbath during the night of Saturday-Sunday, by way of observing the accomplishment in Christ of the Jewish sabbath. The rationalization of an *eighth* day—the day after the seventh—as marking the beginning of a new creation seems to be an idea brought in from Jewish apocalyptic (see Barnabas 15: 8 f.). Rom. 14: 5 f. bears witness to the existence, within the Christian community, of a diversity of views on the observance of holy days. Of the great festivals, the Jewish Passover probably continued to be kept by Christians long after they had found an existence of their own, especially as it lent itself so naturally to a Christian connotation and was bound up with the traditions of the death of Christ (cf. Acts 20: 6; 1 Cor. 5: 7). Other Jewish festivals too must have persisted.[2] In Acts 20: 6 it is implied that Paul observed the Passover (so far as that was possible outside Jerusalem) before leaving Philippi; then, in Acts 20: 16, we find him hurrying so as to reach Jerusalem by Pentecost. Is this in order to celebrate with fellow Christians the Birthday of the Christian Church? Even if it was, it would of necessity have meant also celebrating the festival publicly with the non-Christian Jews: how could that be avoided if one was actually at Jerusalem? There must have been a great deal of overlapping of Jewish feasts and Christian connotations, the one merging into and tending to colour the other. Passover and Pentecost, in their Christian

[1] "Sabbat et Jour du Seigneur" in *New Testament Essays* (as in Note 1, p. 3); cf. C. W. Dugmore (as in Note 1, p. 5), 28, 30.

[2] See D. Daube, "The Earliest Structure of the Gospels", *J.N.T.S.* 5, 3, April 1959, 174*fin.*; E. Lohse in *T.W.N.T.* VI, 49, *Anm.* 35 on the (?Christian) Passover of 1 Cor. 5: 6–8; and (49) on the possibility of Christian Pentecosts outside Jerusalem. See also H. Kretschmar, "Himmelfahrt und Pfingsten", *Zeitschrift für Kirchengeschichte*, 4th series, IV, 1954–5, 209 ff.

forms as Easter and Whitsunday, were destined to form the basis of the "Christian Year".[1] Only when the observance of a certain calendar became bound up with views incompatible with the freedom of the Christian Gospel and the Christian estimate of Christ do we find Paul protesting against it, as in Gal. 4: 10 f.; Col. 2: 16.

The same is true of circumcision. The practice of it alongside of Christian baptism by a judaizing party within the Church only becomes a matter of contention when it encroaches upon the essential Gospel and challenges the uniqueness and finality of Christ (Acts 15, etc.). Paul is prepared to circumcise Timothy so that he may be acceptable to the Jews (Acts 16: 3); but he will not yield for an instant to those who want to treat circumcision as a necessary condition of membership in "God's Israel", over and above incorporation in Christ (Gal. 2: 5; 5: 2; 6: 11–16).

[1] A. A. McArthur, *The Evolution of the Christian Year*, 1953; J. van Goudoever, *Biblical Calendars*, 1959.

II

THE FELLOWSHIP MEAL AND ITS DEVELOPMENTS

1. *"The breaking of the loaf"*

WHATEVER DISTINCTIVE FORMS of Christian worship there were, sprang up side by side with Jewish worship or even within it. What purport to be the beginnings of the distinctive aspects are alluded to in Acts 2: 42: the newly baptized persevered in their faithfulness to the teaching which the apostles gave and to the sharing (κοινωνία), to the breaking of the loaf and to the prayers.

Κοινωνία appears, almost always in the New Testament, to mean "sharing in", or "causing to share in", something or someone, rather than "fellowship" in the sense of mutual or reciprocal companionship (it is only in 1 John 1: 3 that such a sense seems almost inevitable), or in the concrete sense of "a community".[1] What, then, is intended by "the κοινωνία" in Acts 2: 42? Are we to understand that it was a sharing together in the Holy Spirit (cf. 2 Cor. 13: 14)? Or does the word allude to sharing the (sacramental) bread and wine—to "communion" in the liturgical sense? Or is it, rather, an anticipatory reference to the joint-possession of goods by the Christian community?

On the whole, it seems most likely to mean this last.[2] For, although the free gift of the Spirit is indeed mentioned not further away than v. 38, it would be strange to represent "sharing in the Holy Spirit" simply by the absolute, undefined κοινωνία; and the same applies to the suggestion that it means specifically the eucharistic "communion"

---

[1] J. Y. Campbell, "κοινωνία and its cognates in the N.T.", *J.B.L.* 51, 1932, 352 ff. Bo Reicke, *Diakonie, Festfreude und Zelos in Verbindung mit der altchristlichen Agapenfeier*, 1951, 25 f. (κοινωνία is "centripetal"—sharing together—or "centrifugal"—sharing with others, distributing). See also J. G. Davies, *Members One of Another: Aspects of Koinonia*, 1958.

[2] See Bo Reicke, *Glaube und Leben der Urgemeinde: Bemerkungen zu Apg. 1–7*, 1957, 57 f.; H. Schürmann, *Der Abendmahlsbericht, Lukas 22, 7–38*, 1958, 67 f. J. Jeremias, on the other hand, suggests that Acts 2: 42 represents the course of early Christian worship—teaching, fellowship-meal, Eucharist, prayer (*Die Bergpredigt*, 1959).

(in 1 Cor. 10: 16 ff. the definition is much clearer), unless one takes "the breaking of the loaf" as an explanatory phrase in apposition to the κοινωνία. It is simpler to take vv. 44–47 as an expansion and explanation, respectively, of the phrases "the κοινωνία, the breaking of the loaf, and the prayers": the Christians held their goods in common (vv. 44 f.); they "broke bread" together in private houses, that is, first in one home, then in another (v. 46, κατ' οἶκον); and they worshipped and praised God in the Temple (vv. 46 f.). Whenever the Acts account may have been written, there is nothing here that seems incompatible with the very earliest days of the Christian Church in Jerusalem.

But what, then, was this breaking of the loaf? Part of the answer may well be that the sharing of goods just mentioned consisted in large measure in the sharing of food. It was precisely at communal meals that distribution of the necessities of life was made to the indigent. This is borne out by the description in Acts 6: 1 f. of the daily distribution to widows. But one cannot deny the likelihood that, in the very practical and material mutual help and comfort of these community meals, the Christians also realized the spiritual bond uniting them with one another and with Jesus Christ. These occasions must have been more than merely opportunities for the dole. On this reckoning, while "the κοινωνία"—the sharing of goods—included more than food, the meals, conversely, were occasions for something greater and deeper than the mere distribution of food.

To say that in some sense they were also sacred meals does not, however, take us far. For a devout Jew, there was no meal that was not sacred. Indeed, it is an unprofitable question to ask whether "the breaking" (κλάσις) means a merely "secular" act or a ritual "fraction" of the loaf. There is no reason to suppose that a pious Jew would even begin to eat so much as a biscuit without a brief expression of praise and thanks to God as he broke it, even if he were entirely alone.[1] And that "breaking" need only mean the inevitable preliminary to eating, whether for oneself or for distribution among a company of guests, is proved by Isa. 58: 7 (LXX διαθρύπτειν τὸν ἄρτον), Lam. 4: 4

[1] For grace with meals, W. H. Brownlee in his comment (see Note 1, p. 6) on 1 QS vi. 6, compares the practice of the Essenes (Josephus B. J. 2, 131, and possibly Sibyl. iv. 24–26 reflecting Essene influence; c.f. R. H. Charles on iv. 27), the practice of the Pharisees (Aristeas 184 f.; Mishnah, Berakhoth iii), and the practice of Jesus (Matt. 14: 19; 15: 36; 26: 26 f., etc.). But the "grace" in Aristeas is a very odd and very pro-Hellene affair.

(LXX ὁ διακλῶν οὐκ ἔστιν αὐτοῖς), both passages being concerned simply with the provision of food for the needy. In Jer. 16: 7 the LXX actually uses the words ἄρτος, "loaf", and κλᾶν, "to break" in reference to a funeral feast (where also "drinking the cup" is mentioned). That is admittedly a religious, one might say even a ritual, usage; but at least it shows that the words are quite natural outside a strictly sacramental context.[1] Thus, there appears to be nothing essentially significant (for our present purposes) about the word κλάσις, "breaking", even though it (and the concrete noun κλάσμα cognate with it) did rapidly acquire, in Christian usage, a specialized, Eucharistic sense.[2]

Accordingly, it is not in the words, "the breaking of the loaf", but in their context that one must look if one is to detect any further significance in what the Christians did together at their meals. And in fact it does appear from the context that there is more to be said. The very reference to the "exultation and transparent sincerity" with which they took their meals (Acts 2: 46)[3] invites one to look beneath the surface. Is there not something distinctive about these exultantly joyful shared meals?

In the first place, it needs to be remembered that the meals which the disciples had already shared with Jesus before His death must themselves have been memorable. There is nothing that links friends more closely than the sharing of food; and with such a Friend and Master those fellowship meals—even at their most incidental— must have been unforgettable. Then, the traditions told of a spectacular miracle associated with communal feeding—the multiplication of the loaves: seemingly, a foretaste of the banquet of the longed-for Messianic age. Further, astonishing though it might seem, the traditions spoke clearly of meals shared with the Master after His resurrec-

---

[1] In the Talmud "to break (bṣ‘, prs) bread" is a recognized phrase; see S.-B. I, 687, II, 619 f., IV, 621 f.

[2] J. Jeremias, *The Eucharistic Words of Jesus*, Eng. trans., 1955, 83, n. 6, says "The constantly repeated statement that 'breaking of bread' is a term for 'holding a meal' in Jewish sources seems to be an ineradicable misapprehension"; but he allows (*ibid*. 82, n. 5) that the phrase "breaking of bread" can mean the whole ritual at the beginning of the meal—grace, breaking of bread, and distribution. See Behm, in *T.W.N.T.*, III, 728.

[3] See E. Haenchen *in loc.*, who gives good reasons for refusing Jeremias's punctuation (*Eucharistic Words*, as in preceding Note, 84, n. 4) which takes these words with the following words about worship.

tion.[1] All this would be bound to mean that those who had now been baptized into the ownership of Jesus Christ and into His allegiance would find in each meal together at least a very vivid reminder of the One who had so often broken bread with His disciples during His ministry, and who after His resurrection was made known to the two at Emmaus as He broke the bread.

There are many who think that this is where the significance of these meals in the early days of the Palestinian Christians ends. They were simply the fellowship meals of those who shared together in a loyalty to Jesus and His way of life. Any connexion with the Last Supper and the death of Christ belongs, it is alleged, only to the cultic meals of the later Hellenistic Christian communities.[2]

But is it conceivable that that other memory—the memory of the Last Supper—was not also vivid at the very first—indeed, at its most vivid then? The earliest datable account of any Christian meal is in I Cor. 11: 17 ff. If we take *vv.* 23–25, for the moment, as an authentic account of Christian tradition, they would suggest that Christians could hardly have participated in meals together without often recalling at them the close link thus established not only with Christ, but, more explicitly, with His death. To break bread and share a cup together would be to recall not only the unseen presence of the Lord and many meals formerly shared with Him, but also the New Covenant which He had inaugurated at that particular meal in the upper room, in the context of His sacrificial self-surrender at Passover-time, in which they found themselves bonded into God's People. This was the covenant-rite in which they knew themselves to be true Israel—"God's Israel", as it is called in Gal. 6: 16. It was because Jesus was recognized by Christians as God's chosen King, because His death and the solemn meal anticipating it were seen to be the inauguration of the New Covenant sealed by His blood, that every meal together was at least capable of meaning for the Christians a renewal of their commitment as true Israel, as the real People of God. There is no need to believe that every meal explicitly carried this significance: no doubt there was an uninstitutional freedom and flexibility. But if the Pauline tradition is a true one, it is difficult to believe that there was not, from the very first,

[1] See O. Cullmann, e.g. in *Early Christian Worship*, Eng. trans., 1953, 15.
[2] See H. Lietzmann, *Mass and Lord's Supper*, Eng. trans., 1953, 58; A. B. Macdonald, *Christian Worship in the Primitive Church*, 1934; and the bibliography in Bo Reicke, *Diakonie*, etc., as in Note 1, p. 13 ; also (for discussion and criticism) A. J. B. Higgins, *The Lord's Supper in the New Testament*, 1952.

a vivid awareness of this aspect of the Christian breaking of bread also.[1] And to concede this is to recognize something *sacramental* as an original element in distinctively Christian worship.

At this point we must digress a little to ask whether there is anything comparable in pre-Christian practice. The Dead Sea Scrolls include, as is well known, one (usually known as the Manual of Discipline) which throws much light on the practices and institutions of the Jewish Sect who lived at Qumran. It is tempting to find, in the regulations for their community meals, a parallel for the Christian practice. But these meals in fact, so far as the account takes us, were (as Professor H. H. Rowley says) "comparable with the common meals of members of monastic orders today, and no members of these orders would confuse them with the sacrament".[2] It is a striking analogy to the Christian position, that the Sect saw themselves as true Israel.[3] But so far as our present inquiry is concerned, there is nothing recognizably sacramental in the Qumran meal. Is there any other direction in which we may look for a Jewish analogy to the sort of thing which (on the Pauline evidence) we are assuming for the Christians?

In 1889 P. Batiffol published a curious document in Greek, generally known as "Joseph and Aseneth".[4] It is of the nature of what the Jews called *Haggadah*—a narrative romance—built upon the Biblical reference to the marriage between Joseph the Jew and the aristocratic Egyptian lady Aseneth (or Asenath, see Gen. 41: 45). In this story, when Aseneth wants to kiss Joseph he explains that it is not fitting for him to let her do so, since she is a pagan and he a God-fearing man. The important matter for our purposes is the way in which these contrasting ideas are expounded. Joseph is one, he says of himself, who blesses the living God, who eats the blessed bread of life and drinks the blessed cup of immortality and anoints himself with the blessed chrism of incorruptibility. Aseneth, by contrast, is one who blesses the dead, dumb idols, who eats from their table "bread of choking" and drinks from their libations a "cup of ambush", and who anoints herself with the "chrism of destruction". When Aseneth is distressed at this repulse,

---

[1] It is this which, as it seems to me, turns the flank of the Lietzmann position (see preceding Note), which distinguished the bread-breaking, as a mere fellowship-meal of the Palestinian Communities, from the "Pauline" type of Eucharist.

[2] *The Dead Sea Scrolls and the New Testament*, 1957, 16. But, for a different emphasis, see K. G. Kuhn, "The Lord's supper and the Communal Meal at Qumran" in *The Scrolls and the New Testament*, ed. K. Stendahl, Eng. trans., 1958.

[3] See R. Bultmann, *Theologie des Neuen Testaments*[3], 1958, vii.

[4] P. Batiffol, *Studia Patristica*, Fascicule 1, 2, 1889–90.

Joseph prays for her, asking God to renew her with His Holy Spirit, that she may eat God's bread of life and drink His cup of blessing, and be numbered among His chosen people.

Now all this is strikingly reminiscent of Christian Eucharistic language, and, if it is pre-Christian, must point to some conception, otherwise unknown in Judaism, of ritual meals to which one could scarcely deny the term sacramental. Professor G. D. Kilpatrick has suggested[1] that here the curtain is indeed lifted for a moment on some otherwise unknown Jewish religious practice sufficiently similar to the Last Supper for these two to have a common origin independent of the Passover. Professor J. Jeremias also accepts a pre-Christian origin, noting, as particularly significant, the absence of any reference to baptism.[2] But Batiffol himself placed the document as late as the fifth century of the Christian era, and one would need extremely convincing evidence to establish that the story has not been worked over by some Christian hand, or composed by someone at least acquainted with Christianity.[3]

Thus, it is impossible to say with any confidence that there are pre-Christian Jewish analogies to what is indicated in 1 Cor. 11.

Is there, then, any analogy from the pagan world? There were confraternities—$\theta\acute{\iota}\alpha\sigma\omicron\iota$ and $\acute{\epsilon}\tau\alpha\iota\rho\epsilon\hat{\iota}\alpha\iota$—some of them apparently connected with mystery religions; and no doubt their activities included communal meals. Bauer[4] is even able to quote a scholion on Plato which says that the common meals of the Lacedaemonians were called $\phi\iota\lambda\acute{\iota}\tau\iota\alpha$ because they were assemblies of friendship ($\phi\iota\lambda\acute{\iota}\alpha\varsigma$ $\sigma\upsilon\nu\alpha\gamma\omega\gamma\acute{\alpha}$). If the Christian alternative for $\phi\iota\lambda\acute{\iota}\alpha$ is $\acute{\alpha}\gamma\acute{\alpha}\pi\eta$, then these $\phi\iota\lambda\acute{\iota}\tau\iota\alpha$ might be regarded as a striking pagan parallel to

---

[1] *E.T.*, LXIV, 1, Oct. 1952, 4 ff.

[2] See, e.g., his "Die missionarische Aufgabe in der Mischehe (1 Cor. 7: 16)" in *N.T. Studien für Bultmann*, 1954, 256; and *Infant Baptism in the First Four Centuries*, Eng. trans., 1960, 33.

[3] P. Ressler's translation into German, 1928, with brief notes, assigned it to Essene origin; and Kohler, in *The Jewish Encyclopaedia* II, 172–6, treats it as essentially Jewish with only slight Christian revision. K. G. Kuhn (as in Note 2, p. 17) regards it as non-Christian. But E. W. Brooks, *Joseph and Asenath*, 1918, comes down decisively, like Batiffol before him, in favour of its Christian character, adding to the apparently Eucharistic references the evidence of the exaltation of virginity and the prominence of the idea of forgiveness. This edition, incidentally, has a useful account of the extant versions of the work (vii–ix); and is the discussion of the veil (xiv f.) relevant to 1 Cor. 11?

[4] *Wörterbuch zum Neuen Testament*[5], 1958, *s.v.agape*, or Arndt and Gringrich's English edition of Bauer[3], 1957, *Introduction*.

the Christian "love-feast" which itself came to be called ἀγαπη, "a love".[1] Moreover, the process of initiation into the mysteries, which was believed to bring immortality, was at certain points connected with ceremonial eating or drinking.

But beyond this the likenesses do not seem to extend; and the really distinctive thing about the Christian sacramental meal (at any rate, as it is reflected in St. Paul's allusions) is its essentially historical and eschatological character. Looking back to an event of the past, it looks forward to the consummation of God's design; and in the present, at each celebration, it finds a creative meeting of the two.

To the Pauline conception, then, of the Christian communal meal it appears to be impossible to establish any real counterpart either in Judaism or in the pagan world. But does the Pauline tradition itself go back to any actual institution by Jesus? Is it even, broadly speaking, representative of what was done in St. Paul's day by the majority of the Christian congregations scattered over the world? Is it not an invention essentially of Hellenic—not primitive Palestinian—Christianity, or perhaps of Paul himself?

The most realistic answer to this last question is "No". It is difficult to believe that the words "I received from the Lord . . ." (1 Cor. 11: 23) are intended to refer to a direct *vision* accorded privately to the apostle (despite Gal. 1: 12). The correlative verbs παρέλαβον and παρέδωκα naturally apply to the receiving and transmitting of traditions; and it is intrinsically improbable, in any case, that what is here described should be the contents of a vision. "From the Lord" is therefore more naturally interpreted as a reference to apostolic traditions going right back to the Lord Himself. Paul is claiming to be in line with tradition.[2]

But even so, can we believe that such a claim was justifiable? And is not the only other New Testament reference to a dominical command to commemorate the death of Christ—namely Luke 22: 19b—dependent on the Pauline passage?

The authentic character of the Pauline account is not to be so lightly dismissed. As has just been pointed out, the mystery-religion outlook is radically different from what is represented in 1 Cor. 11. If, then, the Pauline words are taken to represent a Hellenic element grafted on to a Palestinian stock, the grafting would need to have been a very extraordinary process. Moreover, it is extremely difficult to imagine St. Paul having the effrontery to claim *as a tradition*

---

[1] See C. Spicq, *Agapè dans le Nouveau Testament*, II, 1959, 347 ff.

[2] See a good discussion in V. Taylor, *Jesus and His Sacrifice*, 1937, 201 ff.

which he had faithfully passed on something which in fact he had imported from paganism. And, further, it is far from certain that the "longer text" of Luke 22: 19 (including the clause just referred to) is either post-Lukan or even merely borrowed by Luke from Paul. A case can be made for the originality of the longer text and for its witnessing independently to the same tradition as is reflected in 1 Cor. 11.[1]

In any case, even if we were to omit the allusion to a dominical command to commemorate the death of Christ, and ignore the peculiarly Lukan and Pauline matter, there would still remain in the narratives of the Last Supper alike in Paul, Luke, Matthew and Mark a reference to the blood of Christ shed for many; and it is exceedingly difficult to escape the conclusion that in all available references to the traditions there is at least a linking of the idea of the death of Christ on behalf of others with this fellowship meal. And although many scholars find difficulty in including among the aboriginal elements of the tradition the description of the blood of Christ as "*covenant*-blood",[2] even this seems, after all, to represent a quite possible Aramaic phrase;[3] and certainly nothing is more obviously natural to Old Testament thought than the idea of the Covenant between God and His People, which was one day to be renewed in a deeper, more inward, more effective way (Jer. 31: 31).

If, then, the Pauline and Lukan accounts of the Last Supper do represent in the main not a recent Hellenizing development but a primitive tradition, then from the very first "the breaking of the loaf" (which in itself, as we have argued, need be no more than a Semitic phrase for starting a meal) could always for the Christians have been associated with the covenant renewed by God in the death of Christ. This removes the grounds for chronological or topographical distinc-

[1] See Jeremias, *The Eucharistic Words of Jesus* (as in Note 2, p. 15), 87 ff.; and H. Schürmann, *Der Einsetzungsbericht*, 1955. The late Dr. T. W. Manson, on the other hand, thought that the longer text, though indeed Lukan, arose from Luke's own augmentation of his material by a liturgical phrase: Luke 22: 14–18 and 21–38 is "L" material, into which Luke himself has inserted 19, 20—liturgical words which he may have learned from Paul. I do not find Jeremias' explanation convincing. But I do not think that it is necessary to regard the "interpolation" as unhistorical, still less as post-Lukan. Schürmann's conclusions, based on very detailed statistical examination of the context, are worthy of respect.

[2] See, e.g., E. Lohse, *Märtyrer und Gottesknecht*, 1955, 126, and the bibliography in H. Schürmann (as in Note 1 above), 95, nn. 324 ff. See also the discussion in W. D. Davies, *Paul and Rabbinic Judaism*, 1948, 244 ff.

[3] J. A. Emerton, "The Aramaic underlying *to haima mou tes diathekes* in Mk. xiv. 24", *J.T.S.* n.s. VI, 2, Oct. 1955, 238 ff.

tions, such as Lietzmann made in *Mass and Lord's Supper*, between a primitive Palestinian fellowship-meal and a sacramental, Hellenistic "Eucharist". The sharing of the bread and wine, with an expression of praise to God for what He had done in the death and resurrection of Christ, may from the first have been known as a means of renewing union with the risen Christ. Here, in short, may have been from the first a real sacrament—the use of material things, the bread and wine, in the context of the mighty work of God in Christ, in such a way that the worshippers are confronted with God Himself, brought to a fresh decision before Him, and so enabled to enter into a relationship with Him.

It does not follow that every reference to the breaking of bread, in circumstances such that no special mention was made of the death of Christ, is necessarily a reference to a sacrament. Even the Pauline phrase "whenever you eat this loaf and drink the cup, you declare the Lord's death . . ." (1 Cor. 11: 26) need not compel us to a pedantic literalism turning every Christian act of feeding into a "Eucharist". Admittedly, if a devout Jew always "said grace" before eating, it is difficult to imagine a devout Christian not using a distinctively Christian form of grace; and, if so, it is a question exactly where one draws the line between a Christian grace and a memorial of the death of Christ by which the occasion becomes a sacrament. But the point is that a clearly sacramental use, whether invariably present or not, does seem to have existed from the earliest days among the Christians.

If we may digress for a moment on the subject of grace before meals, the directions in *Didache* 9, 10 look uncommonly as though they related simply to an extended grace before and after a meal. And to such there appears to be reference also in 1 Tim. 4: 5. There we find a repudiation of some false teaching which evidently included elaborate food-taboos; and as against this teaching, it is affirmed that everything created by God is good, "and nothing is to be rejected, if it is accepted with thanksgiving (εὐχαριστία); for it is consecrated (ἁγιάζεται) through the word of God and prayer (ἔντευξις)". Here "the word of God" is perhaps a reference to the divine declaration of the goodness of created things (Gen. 1: 31); and the prayer is the prayer of thanksgiving over food (see B. S. Easton *in loc.*). This passage from 1 Tim. has passed into many academic graces used before dinner in the ancient Universities, in such forms as *sanctifica dona tua per verbum et orationem*. But Justin, *Apol.* i. 66, draws a parallel between the incarnation "through the word of God" and the transformation of the eucharistic elements over which thanksgiving has been made "through the word of prayer which comes from God"; and it seems possible that already by the time of 1 Tim., although no such transformation was yet imagined, the grace pronounced over the food was itself regarded as God's divinely given word. In that case, the phrase means "through the word of God, *namely* prayer". In either case, ἔντευξις, more narrowly "intercession", seems to be used here in its more general sense of "prayer".[1]

Thus, to return to the main issue, it is impossible, at an early period, to draw hard and fast lines between "mere" eating and "sacramental" participation, between mere grace before meals and Eucharist. What does seem to be justified is the recognition of the early existence of a sacramental "Eucharist". A good case may no doubt be made for the *Didache's* references being to a non-sacramental meal (possibly, as Audet and others before him suggest,[2] preliminary to a "Eucharist" proper); and certainly it would be almost ludicrous to hold that when, on the storm-tossed ship, St. Paul took bread and broke it before the whole company (Acts 27: 35), he must have been doing something "sacramental". But it is another matter when at Troas a body of Christians assembles on a Sunday[3] expressly to break bread (Acts 20: 7). There it seems highly probable that something more than a "mere meal" is intended.

In the New Testament there is very little trace of any technical name such as "Eucharist" or "Holy Communion" to distinguish the rite. Indeed, the only names there are describe, rather, the larger context from which the Eucharist proper was ultimately to be distinguished. In 1 Cor. 11: 20, reference is made to a "Lord's supper", κυριακὸν δεῖπνον; a supper, that is, associated with Jesus as Lord, and contrasted (in this instance) with the selfish use of food as "one's own supper" (*v.* 21). Again, it is probable that in Jude 12 the ἀγάπαι in which the antinomians are shamelessly enjoying themselves are the Christian love-feasts. If so, this is the only instance in the New Testament of this term (unless in 2 Pet. 2: 13 ἀγάπαις is the right reading, rather than ἀπάταις). In the letters of Ignatius of Antioch, however, this technical term is evidently well established, as is also the technical

---

[1] It occurs only once elsewhere in the N.T.—in 1 Tim. 2: 1; but see Bauer or Arndt and Gringrich *s.v.* Does it conceivably refer to the eucharistic intercession, *during* which thanks would also be offered?

[2] J.-P. Audet, *La Didachè*, 1958, 415. Before him, see (e.g.) Lietzmann (as in Note 2, p. 16), and G. Bornkamm, *Das Ende des Gesetzes*, 1952, 123 ff.

[3] Or on the night ending the sabbath (see Note 1, p. 11).

use of the verb ἀγαπᾶν in the sense "to keep a love-feast" (it is unlikely that this is the meaning of the verb in John 13: 1). (Why the noun ἀγάπη, "love", ever came to be adopted for this sense of "loving-*feast*" is obscure, unless the pagan parallel cited above (p. 23) throws any light—and, in any case, there the word is not φιλίαι, "loves", which it would be if the parallel were exact.)[1]

But even if, as yet, there was no technical name for the sacrament—the Eucharist proper within the love-feast—there is no reason (if the argument so far is on the right lines) to doubt its existence. How often, then, was it celebrated? The Last Supper, whether a Passover or not,[2] was at least at the paschal season and was clearly related to the Passover; and Passover was an annual festival. Did Jesus then intend the breaking of the loaf in memory of Him to be no more than an annual act?[3] The only actual phrase of frequency associated with the Lord's Supper in the whole New Testament, in 1 Cor. 11: 26, is unfortunately a relative phrase—"as often as . . .". If we take "eating this bread and drinking the cup" to refer to ordinary meals, then the memorial is intended to attach to every meal taken by Christians together (even if, as has been already remarked, this would still not need to be pedantically pressed); but if, as seems far more probable, it refers to a special occasion for worship, then we are no nearer to determining how frequently that happened.

Almost all we have to go by, therefore (so far as New Testament evidence goes) is the fact that in Acts 20: 7 coming together on the first day of the week to break bread is mentioned as though it were a matter of course. But a weekly "coming together" is further suggested by the fact that in 1 Cor. 16: 1 f. St. Paul instructs the Corinthians to make an allocation of money out of their savings for the Jerusalem poor every Sunday (κατὰ μίαν σαββάτου). In *Didache* 14: 1 the injunction to come together every "Lord's day" to break bread is explicit: but the date of this section of the *Didache* (as indeed of any part of that writing) is uncertain.[4] The term "the Lord's day" occurs once in the New

---

[1] See C. Spicq, as in Note 1, p. 19.

[2] For the thorny question as to the date of the Last Supper, and whether it was a Passover or not, see, among very many others, J. Jeremias (as in Note 2, p. 15), Ch. I; A. J. B. Higgins, as in Note 2. p. 16; A. Jaubert, "La date de la dernière Cène", *Revue de l'histoire des religions*, CXLVI, 140 ff.; M. Black, "The Arrest and Trial of Jesus and the Date of the Last Supper" in *New Testament Essays*, as in Note 1, p. 3, 19 ff.

[3] See A. J. B. Higgins, as in Note 2, p. 16.

[4] See J.-P. Audet, as in Note 2, p. 22, *in loc.*

Testament itself: that the seer of the Apocalypse finds himself in the Spirit (? in a trance or ecstasy) on the Lord's day (Rev. 1: 10) suggests that it was a day for worship; and the whole of the Apocalypse is indeed full of the sights and sounds of worship.

In any case, moreover, Jewish Christians in the early days would, as we have seen, still have kept the sabbath; and the distinctively Christian act of worship may well have followed on the night of the sabbath or in the small hours of the Sunday (which, after all, was not yet a holiday, and could not normally be a whole day of worship). Sabbath was, for Jews, especially a memorial of the creation. The *new* creation in Jesus Christ would suitably have been celebrated weekly, in connexion with the sabbath, or at the breaking of the day of the resurrection.[1]

Thus, it may certainly be said that the Jewish sabbath provided a strong incentive to the Christians for a weekly Eucharist, although it is impossible to find any secure evidence for it as an invariable practice, still less for any hard and fast rule to this effect. We must be content to say that it is likely enough to have been a weekly practice; and a little later, outside the New Testament, we have (besides the *Didache* just cited) Pliny's famous *stato die* (10. 96–7), Barnabas 15: 9, and Justin (*Apol.* I. 67.3).

To sum up thus far, there appears to be sufficient evidence for believing that, from the earliest days, a sacrament such as came to be called the Holy Communion or Eucharist was celebrated, probably weekly, and usually in the context of a communal meal.

2. *The president*

If we turn now to the conduct of eucharistic worship, in the first place, it is unfortunately impossible to be certain who presided. It is natural to assume that an apostle would preside (or at least be invited to preside), if present. The prestige of the Twelve, as eye-witnesses commissioned by the Lord to give evidence of the Gospel facts, may be assumed to have set them at the head of a congregation assembled for worship. (It does not follow, although this is often too lightly assumed, that the same prestige necessarily put them at the administrative head of any community—still less that the dominical commission itself included any such responsibility.) The same no doubt applied to St. Paul, where his apostleship was recognized, although, as is evident from 2 Cor., that was not everywhere. Failing an apostle, the president would presumably be one of the elders of the local congregation, but

[1] See Note 1, p. 11.

not necessarily always the same one. Even much later, Justin, *Apol.* I.65, simply alludes to the president (ὁ προεστώς), as though there might be different persons on different occasions. One of the theories of the origin of episcopacy looks primarily to the Eucharist.[1] On this showing, the celebrant might have been the "bishop"—the chief elder-overseer (or presbyter-bishop), who would be assisted by the other elder-overseers (or presbyter-bishops) and the deacons. But in fact it seems reasonable to find the functions of these ministries in several different activities concurrently—not only in liturgical leadership but also in pastoral and administrative responsibilities. In the Pastoral Epistles, nothing is said specifically about worship among the qualifications of presbyter-overseers and deacons.

3. *Eucharistic procedure*

What actually took place at a Eucharist? No doubt the answer to that question would vary at different periods and in different areas. In the earliest days and in Judaea—to judge from Acts—it seems to have been something like the following. The Christians met together daily, weekly, or at irregular intervals, to enjoy the companionship of meals together (as also to supply the needs of the indigent, Acts 2: 45, 6: 1).[2] They shared their food with one another in a spirit of exultant joy (because of the triumph of Christ and its shortly expected consummation, and because of their mutual bond with one another in Christ), and with transparent sincerity (a mark of their prevailing intimacy and freedom from guilty secrets)—Acts 2: 46.

To such meals (usually in the evening, or at night, or even in the small hours, for the reasons already given) we may assume that each member would bring his own contribution according to his means. Slaves might bring the remains of feasts at which they had been waiters; the better-off might buy something for the occasion; many a housewife would see what she could find in the larder. And it was most probably at the beginning of such a meal—a real meal, for the satisfaction of hunger and for the assistance of the indigent—that the president, whoever he might be that day, would take a loaf or biscuit, and, as he held it, would burst into a flood of praise. He would praise

---

[1] See, e.g., H. F. Hamilton, *The People of God*, II, 1912, 87 ff.; and, for a summary, T. O. Wedel, *The Coming Great Church*, Eng. ed., 1947, 136.

[2] Bo Reicke (as in Note 2, p. 13), 158 f., compares the phrase for the indigent in 1 Cor. 11: 22 (οἱ μὴ ἔχοντες) with exactly the same phrase in a description of a festal distribution of largesse in Neh. 8: 10 (LXX 2 Esdras 18: 10 οἱ μὴ ἔχοντες).

or "bless" God, both for His wonderful works of creation and for His mighty deeds in history; but, most especially, for what He had done in Jesus Christ, and what He would do ultimately through Him. And here reference would be made to what Jesus Himself had said about His body and blood as He handled the bread at the Last Supper in the upper room. There might also be petitions and intercessions.

This rendering of praise—this blessing or "eulogy"—might be short or long: it rested with the president. (By the time of the *Didache* (10: 7), if indeed the Eucharistic prayer is meant, ordinary presidents were wisely held within bounds by a fixed form: only "prophets" were allowed free rein.) As he concluded, he would break the single loaf or biscuit for distribution, and there might be at this point explicit allusion to the idea of the many fragments all belonging to the single loaf—a parable and pledge of the union of the many worshippers as parts of a single loaf, as limbs of a single body (1 Cor. 10: 17), a foretaste of the final assembling of the scattered fragments of God's Israel at the consummation (*Didache* 9: 4, 10: 5, cf. the Jewish prayer for the gathering of Israel, in the '*amidah*, i.e. "standing", prayer in synagogue worship).[1]

This done, the meal would proceed. There would, no doubt, be informal conversation, grave and gay, the exchange of news and views, the discussion of problems and anxieties, of hopes and fears.

Then, after supper, came a second blessing or thanksgiving, this time not over the bread but over a cup, with appropriate allusions and, again, with the appropriate part of the narrative of the upper room and, probably, allusion to the expectations of the future. The president, it seems, would then take a sip from the cup and pass it round for each in turn to drink from.

Most of this is deduction, partly from known Jewish practice, partly from the New Testament narratives of the upper room. It must be remembered, however, that those narratives describe something that took place at Passover time, and it is possible that only at Passover time would the Christian communal meals have approximated at all closely

---

[1] W. Bauer (as in Note 4, p. 18) *s.v. ἄρτος* (or, in Arndt and Gringrich's translation, xiii) cites Diog. Laert. 8, 35, where Pythagoras says that the one loaf (εἷς ἄρτος) has served as a bond between friends. On *Didache* 9: 4 see E. R. Goodenough, "John a Primitive Gospel", *J.B.L.* 64, 1945, 145 ff., C. F. D. Moule, "A note on *Did.* 9: 4", *J.T.S.* n.s. VI. 2, Oct. 1955, 240 ff., H. Riesenfeld, "Das Brot von den Bergen, zu Didache 9, 4", *Eranos* 45, 1956, 142 ff., L. Cerfaux, "La Multiplication des Pains dans la Liturgie de la Didache", *Studia Biblica et Orientalia*, 1959, II. N.T., 375 ff.

to the Jewish Passover pattern. There is some reason to believe that I Cor. 11 was itself written at the Passover season;[1] and it follows that the procedure at meals at other seasons was not necessarily so paschal in character, although the original event, being itself paschal both by chronology and significance, may be assumed to have coloured all procedure to some extent. Reference has already been made to the absence of all mention of a paschal lamb at the Last Supper itself, as distinct from its preparation (and compare the passing allusion in I Cor. 5: 7).

At all events, that devout Jews never began a meal without breaking the foodstuff with a "benediction"—that is, a rendering of praise to God—seems clear; and, equally, that the host shared the initial piece of food with his guests. That at a special meal such as that of the Passover, or even that of a voluntary religious group of associates (a so-called *haburah* or "fellowship"), there was a cup at the end, with a thanksgiving over it, seems equally well established.[2] Whether the normal Jewish practice was for each guest at this point to drink from his own cup, or whether it was to share in a single cup, is disputed.[3] The traditions about the upper room all agree that Jesus passed the cup to the disciples (possibly even refraining Himself): and it is not unreasonable to believe that this passing round of a single cup, whether a peculiarity or not, was perpetuated at Christian gatherings thereafter.

If this is a fair reconstruction of primitive Christian practice in the Judaean areas, it means that the essentials were the breaking and sharing of a foodstuff at the beginning of the meal, and the sharing of a cup at the end, both with benedictions. Moreover, the benedictions included reference to Jesus and His atoning death with eager expectation of the longed-for consummation in the future; at any rate, this is not only *a priori* probable but seems to be indicated for St. Paul's

[1] T. W. Manson. *J.T.S.*, XLVI, 1945, 8.

[2] D. Daube, *The New Testament and Rabbinic Judaism*, 1956, 330 f., makes a case for "the cup of blessing" being the third of four cups prescribed for the *Passover-eve* service. In that case, it would be the fourth cup that Jesus (perhaps) abjured in the words "I will not drink henceforth . . .".

[3] Jeremias (as in Note 2, p. 15), 44, holds that the shared cup was normal. *Contra* H. Schürmann, *Der Paschamahlbericht*, 1952, 60 (citing modern writers *pro* and *contra*), and S.-B. IV, 58 f., 62. But the notion of a "loving-cup"—a single cup shared by all—may be assumed to be instinctive and universal, and it is not easy to believe that it was abnormal at Passover. That it was at some period avoided for hygienic reasons (S.-B. IV, 59 *a*) only reinforces the impression that it was otherwise normal.

tradition, which he may have received from Palestinian sources (1 Cor. 11: 26).

It is to be noted here that the words "Do this . . ." (1 Cor. 11: 24 f.; Luke 22: 19), even if a genuine tradition of the words of Jesus, are unlikely to represent a dominical command to perform the *actions of breaking and distributing*. As G. Dix and others have observed, no devout Jew would need such a command: he would naturally do this whenever a communal meal took place.[1] The operative words, therefore, must be "in remembrance of me". It is not that the disciples are commanded to break bread and share wine. The former they would do every time they ate; the latter, at least on festal or community occasions. It must be, rather, that the command bids them, whenever they do this, to do it "*with special intention*".

There is no evidence within the New Testament of a tradition that any "manual acts", in imitation of what Jesus may have done in the upper room, were regarded as a *sine qua non* for a celebration of the Lord's Supper. But when Christianity left prevailingly Judaean surroundings, whether in Galilee or at Syrian Antioch, or further out in the pagan world, as at Corinth and other Pauline churches, the typically Judaean "breaking of the bread" might not be supported by social custom; and here, to judge again from 1 Cor. 11: 24 and perhaps from the account of the meeting at Troas in Acts 20: 7, 11, it may have been deliberately perpetuated, as a re-enactment of what Jesus did at the Last Supper. Similarly, if the procedure with the cup, and the stage at which it occurred, were maintained unchanged on Gentile soil, that, too, might be for specifically Christian reasons, in places where there was not the further support of antecedent custom. But the nature of the communal meal lying between these two points may there have been more akin to that of the pagan θίασοι and ἑταιρεῖαι such as were associated with mystery-religions or political movements, than to that of the Jewish ḥaburoth.

It may have been precisely this that led the way to the gross abuses which appear to have necessitated ultimately the segregation of the breaking of bread and the sharing of the cup from the real meal so that they became a separate, self-contained ritual. This separation of common fellowship from sacramental rite is utterly alien to St. Paul's mind (cf. 1 Cor. 11), and, when it did come, must have been accepted only as the less of two evils. When the divorce was effected, the ἀγάπη, or "love-feast", evidently continued independently as a separate entity.

[1] G. Dix, *The Shape of the Liturgy*, 1945, 55 f.; Jeremias (as in Note 2, p. 15), 126.

There is no direct evidence from the New Testament of this step having yet been taken. But sooner or later it was accomplished; and there is all too clear evidence for the abuse of the common meal, in 1 Cor. 11 and perhaps also in 2 Pet. 2: 13 and Jude 12. And indirect evidence that the segregation had already taken place before the end of the New Testament period may be derived from a comparison of the different accounts of the words of Jesus at the Last Supper. In 1 Cor. 11: 25 and Luke 22: 20 the position of the cup "after supper" is expressly mentioned; and in neither of these places have the words over the cup been brought into precise parallelism with the words over the bread.[1] By contrast, the Markan and Matthean forms, where the parallelism is exact, may reflect an assimilation of the cup-saying to the bread-saying resulting from their later juxtaposition when the intervening meal or ἀγάπη had dropped out.[2]

Finally, it must be noted that no "general confession" is clearly evidenced for New Testament Eucharists. The Lord's Prayer contains

---

[1] If the earliest "cup words" were in some form *other* than "This is my blood . . .", then it seems to me more than ever impossible to be sure that the mention of blood at this point proves that the wine used must have been *red* (which, in turn, is said to indicate a paschal meal). The whole of such a construction is conjectural. See Jeremias, 29; D. Daube (as in Note 2, p. 11), 176—but he exercises great caution.

[2] A third step in the evolution has been suggested, which, however, seems very far-fetched. The suggestion is that a third stage is represented by the language of John 6 (assuming that this is consciously Eucharistic), where the words are not "*body* and blood" but "*flesh* and blood". The special significance of this—supposing that it is to be fitted into this evolutionary scheme—could be that, in the original sayings, neither "body" nor "blood" was strictly *sacrificial* in connotation. They both represented the self-surrender of Jesus, in terms (it might be) of the suffering Servant of Isa. 53, but not in terms of *cultic* sacrifice. The mention of the covenant, however, when associated with "blood" (whether in the original words of Jesus or, as some hold, later and at a non-Jewish stage—but see Notes 2, 3, p. 20), would invest the word "blood" with definitely sacrificial associations; and the approximation of the cup-saying to the bread-saying would then alter the bread-saying so that it, too, took on a sacrificial meaning: and the substance of an animal sacrifice is *flesh* and blood.

But the Johannine use of σάρξ, "flesh", arises almost certainly not from any such process as is here suggested but from a motive which runs right through the Gospel and the Johannine Epistles—that of affirming the reality of the incarnation as against "docetist" theories (cf. Heb. 2: 14). Moreover, it is simpler (as has been observed, p. 20) to regard the covenant-theme as an original element.

But the assimilation of the two sayings to one another *in their essential structure* may well be still the result of the approximation of the two when the intervening meal had been removed.

a prayer for forgiveness, I Tim. 5: 20 may be thought to imply public penance, and Jas. 5: 16 alludes to mutual confession: that is all.

4. *Sacramental theory*

There is within the New Testament no clear definition of a sacrament. But it is possible to deduce from St. Paul's epistles the principles of sacramental worship, at any rate as he saw them. St. Paul's clearly sacramental viewpoint emerges, albeit incidentally, from his discussion in I Corinthians of food offered to idols. What were Christians to do, when the only meat obtainable, other than the "cosher" meat in the Jewish market (from which they may have been boycotted), had all been ritually offered to pagan gods? That (as I Cor. 8 shows) was a question put to St. Paul by his Christian friends in Corinth, though by some it had already been answered. There were enlightened, sophisticated, comparatively intellectual Christians there who said "Eat it by all means: it is not altered by being offered to an idol". But St. Paul is more careful. He readily agrees (I Cor. 8: 4–6, 10: 19) that there has been no transformation in the meat itself: an idol is nothing, and as far as that goes, we are neither the better nor the worse for eating the meat. But, he says, it is vital that our freedom from superstitious scruples should not be allowed to force the pace for a weaker mentality and thus injure a fellow-Christian's conscience. One must consider not merely one's own position but one's influence on others less emancipated (I Cor. 8: 7–13, 10: 23 ff.). Besides—and this is where the sacramental principle emerges—though the *meat* is not changed, the use of it with a particular intention and in a particular context may and can affect our relationship with the unseen powers of evil and good: there may, that is, be a change of *relation* even though there is no change of *material* (I Cor. 10: 20–22). And St. Paul invokes the analogy of the Eucharist: "the cup of blessing"—that is, the cup over which we bless God—does it not involve participation in the blood of Christ? The loaf which we break, does it not mean participation in the body of Christ (I Cor. 10: 16)? That is to say, the use of bread and wine in a context of Christian worship and (as we have seen) in relation to Christ's death effects an actual participation in Christ's sacrificed life—and St. Paul's readers evidently know it. It actually unites the worshippers with Christ—and with one another: the single loaf broken up and shared is a means of the joint-participation of the many members in the life of a single body (I Cor. 10: 17).

And so vividly real is this for St. Paul that, in I Cor. 11, he is able to say that abuse of this relationship (as by a selfish indifference to the needs of others—a failure to recognize the body corporate which has been created by the surrendered body of Christ) brings illness or even death, so deadly earnest is the apostle's attitude to the real presence of the Lord and the dynamic meaning of a sacramental relationship. It is in this context that we find the first explicit mention in the New Testament of self-examination as a preparation for Communion.[1] Here at least there is direct evidence of the view that "Christian corporate worship is above all the Body of Christ taking visible form".[2]

Thus, although we have no information within the New Testament about the details of procedure, which, indeed, may not have been fixed and standardized so early, this, at all events, can be said: that at least for St. Paul the Lord's Supper was no mere recalling of a memory from the past, nor only a looking forward to the future, but a potent means of present contact with the risen Lord.

If such use of 1 Cor. 8 and 10 as well as 11 is justified, this interpretation of the Eucharist as more than bare recollection or anticipation rests on a firmer foundation than merely the meaning of $\epsilon\iota\varsigma$ $\tau\grave{\eta}\nu$ $\grave{\epsilon}\mu\grave{\eta}\nu$ $\grave{a}\nu\acute{a}\mu\nu\eta\sigma\iota\nu$. It has been argued by Jeremias[3] that this means "in order to remind God" of what Jesus has done. This is far from convincing;[4] and even the observation[5] that, for the Hebrews generally, "remembrance" tended to mean something more dynamic (something nearer to "re-presentation") than mere mental recollection may, while true, not take us all the way. But the "sacramentalism" of St. Paul's outlook does seem to emerge from the context as a whole.

And it is plausible to see a similarly vivid awareness of the meaning of this sacrament reflected in such passages as John 6 and Heb. 10. In John 6, while a false, materialistic parody of sacramentalism is repudiated—"the flesh profiteth nothing: the words that I speak unto you, they are spirit and they are life"—there is also the daring language about eating the flesh and drinking the blood of the Son of Man. This language (shocking in the extreme to Jewish sensibilities about the

[1] See C. F. D. Moule, "The Judgment theme in the Sacraments", in *The Background of the New Testament and its Eschatology* (*in hon.* C. H. Dodd, ed. W. D. Davies and D. Daube), 1956, 454 ff.

[2] E. Schweizer, "Worship in the New Testament", *The Reformed and Presbyterian World*, XXIV, 5, March 1957, 199 (Eng. trans. of *Der Gottesdienst im N.T.*, 1958).

[3] As in Note 2, p. 15; 159 ff.

[4] See, e.g., D. Jones, *J.T.S.* n.s. VI. 2, Oct. 1955, 183 ff.

[5] G. Dix (as in Note 1, p. 28), 161 f.

drinking of blood) seems to mean two things, among much else: first, that the real incarnation must be taken with brutal seriousness and not refined away into some sort of "docetic" notions; and secondly, that salvation is not merely by seeing and listening and learning but by "assimilating" Christ: by so taking into one's life the surrendered life of Christ that new life and strength come into one's character. That such a message should be attached to the narrative of physical, material feeding strongly suggests its application to the eucharistic feast.

In Heb. 10: 26–31, in a context which seems to be best explained as concerned with the mortal danger of apostasy—a lapse back from Christianity into non-Christian Judaism—the fatal step is described in terms of treading underfoot the Son of God and treating as "common" (un-sacred) the blood of the covenant by which one had been dedicated. This, though not demonstrably eucharistic, is reminiscent of the eucharistic context of 1 Cor. 11 where (although there it is not apostasy but common gluttony and selfishness) the sin is a failure "to recognize the body"—the body of Christ surrendered for us and that body, which is the Church, which was thereby created. Heb. 6: 3 ff. seems to be, like Heb. 10: 26 ff., a reference to apostasy, but in terms of a baptismal background.

Elsewhere in Hebrews, the passage most often associated with the eucharist is 13: 10 ff. But it is questionable whether in fact the reference is not even wider, although it quite possibly includes eucharistic worship. The description of praise and almsgiving, in 13: 15 f., as acceptable sacrifices is typical of a widespread religious idea ranging from the Old Testament (possibly actually Hos. 14: 2 here cited) and the Apocrypha, Philo, and the Qumran documents[1] to the more refined and philosophic pagan writers.[2] It stands for a recognition that true worship of God is independent of material sacrifices or at any rate on a deeper level than they. And in the present context this idea gains point if it is correct to see in the whole epistle to the Hebrews an earnest exhortation addressed to Christians who had come out from Judaism. They are urged to recognize that, by leaving Judaism, they have not been bereft of priesthood and sacrifice nor unchurched. They have the philosopher's "inward" worship, and more. They have more than all that Judaism and the philosophers put together could offer—they have

---

[1] See Note 2, p. **6**. But for this sect the substitution of morality, etc., for animal sacrifice may have been regarded as only a *temporary* expedient.

[2] See, e.g., references given by H. Windisch *in loc.* (Lietzmann's *Handbuch zum N.T.*).

the realities of which these were only the adumbration or the hints. If that is the force of "we *have* an altar" in 13: 10, the altar in question is most naturally interpreted as primarily the cross (or the "heavenly altar" upon which the sacrifice of the cross is offered); and the Christian's "eating" from that altar must be his entire relationship with Christ, including, but going beyond, the offering of praise and almsgiving, and including other expressions of that relationship besides the Holy Communion, however central that might be. Participation in Christ's once-for-all sacrifice is the inward meaning of all that the Christians do.

This is only one of many interpretations. One of the exegetical problems involved in reaching a decision is to determine what is meant by those who serve the tabernacle having no right to eat from it. In the interpretation just put forward the passage is taken to mean simply that there can be no access to the Gospel of the death of Christ (no access to the "heavenly altar") for non-Christian Jews (described as "those who serve the tabernacle" because Judaism is, throughout this epistle, described in terms of the Pentateuchal assembly in the wilderness, of which the priests, who serve the tabernacle, are the most privileged). It has been suggested alternatively that the whole phrase means "we have a *sacrifice* [sic] like that from which in the Mosaic Law even the *priests* are not allowed to eat"—that is, Christ's self-sacrifice is comparable to the solemn sacrifice of the day of Atonement, of which no part was eaten, even by the priests (Lev. 6: 30). But this does violence to the meaning of θυσιαστήριον (which means altar, not sacrifice), as well as introducing a curiously oblique reference to the nature of the atonement. Again, the allusion has been interpreted more specifically as an allusion to the Eucharist. But there is nothing to compel one to this conclusion; and it seems more natural (assuming the situation suggested in the previous paragraph) to see in the whole passage (*vv.* 10–16) a reply for the Christians to give to the non-Christian Jews who taunt them with having lost priesthood and sacrifice. On the contrary, they are to say, we *have* an altar, and one from which even the most privileged among you, who boast of your sacrificial system, are not yet qualified to eat. In parenthesis, *vv.* 11–14 recognize that such a claim will lead to ostracism; and the ritual of the day of Atonement is used as a symbol for Christ's expulsion and thus as a ground for accepting this consequence: let us go outside the camp with Jesus, who, like the victims of that sin-offering (Lev. 16: 27), was taken "outside". Then the apologia continues: we *have* sacrifices of our own to offer also—

33

those of praise (the "fruit-offering" from our lips)[1] and of almsgiving and other good deeds. These are the sacrifices which really please God.[2]

There is no need to find in these latter phrases a doctrine of meritorious "good works", as though these human "offerings" were effective for atonement; the point is simply that the Christian "sacrifice" of praise and gifts is pleasing to God rather than the animal sacrifices which the readers of Hebrews are taunted for having abandoned.

If, then, specific allusions to the Holy Communion in Hebrews are uncertain and at best scanty, yet the principles of Christian worship are there. And among these a further principle, of wide influence, has yet to be mentioned, and one which is particularly prominent in this epistle. Jesus is described as the High Priest who has entered heaven on our behalf. The analogy seems, again, to be the day of Atonement—the only day in the Jewish year when the inner sanctuary, the "holy of holies", was penetrated into by any human being. Only on that day the High Priest, and he alone and not without elaborate precautions, entered into the august presence represented by the "mercy seat", the symbolic throne of God on the top of the ark (Lev. 16: 13). The whole assembly outside may be imagined to have waited eagerly until he reappeared (Lev. 16: 20). This analogy is magnificently applied to Christ's glorification and exaltation and looked-for reappearance. Having offered Himself (the "Body" prepared for Him by God—Ps. 40 in the version in which it is quoted in Heb. 10: 5), He has entered heaven (9: 24), there to make intercession for us (7: 25); and thence He will reappear, apart from sin, to bring salvation (9: 28). The fact of the death and resurrection of Christ, truly man, is our confidence before God; and whatever Christian worship is offered on earth is linked with that which is beyond the veil, where Christ represents us before the heavenly throne (9: 24, etc.: cf. 10: 19–22). It may therefore even be said that, in a manner of speaking, the worshipping Church is already united with the whole company of heaven: Christians have already come to mount Sion and are there at worship with the angels in festal array and the whole community of the firstborn (12: 22 ff.).

[1] Cf. 1 QS 9: 4–5; and the liturgical terms used metaphorically by St. Paul (see Epilogue, pp. 78 f.).

[2] B. Reicke (as in Note 2, p. 13), 25 f., plausibly associates the κοινωνία of Heb. 13: 16 (as in Acts 2: 42, see above, p. 13) with the distribution of food actually at the fellowship meal. He is less convincing when he argues (pp. 37 f.) that in Jas. 1: 27, 2: 16 the "religion" (θρησκεία) and the phrases "Go in peace, be warmed and filled" are all to be associated with the corporate worship of the community.

This brings us to the well-known but remarkable fact that 1 Clement (which may date from within the New Testament period) presents many striking parallels to the thought and language of Hebrews, and contains allusions which it is difficult to believe are not eucharistic. And it is far from impossible that, even if the writer to the Hebrews is not attempting to reproduce liturgical language, he is in fact so steeped in it that it echoes through his mind. And it may even be that the resemblances between Hebrews and 1 Clement reflect the manner of celebrating Holy Communion in first-century Rome which was known to both these writers.[1] To acknowledge this is not to go back on the conclusion that Heb. 13: 10 is not to be limited to the Eucharist.

Two further observations must here be made. First, about sacrifice or offering or oblation. Of recent years renewed prominence has been given to the "offertory" at the Eucharist in Anglican Churches. For many generations, before the present time, the placing of the bread and wine on the table had been (and in many churches still is) obscurely performed by the celebrant in the sanctuary so as to be scarcely noticed by the congregation, in contrast to the collecting of the money, which is congregational and obvious and terminates with a procession of collectors to the sanctuary. But originally the bread and wine really came from the congregation: they were themselves contributed by the participants, and might be regarded as a symbol of the bringing to God of the whole stuff of daily life: representing, as they did, the human toil and labour of the week, they could be regarded as a kind of first-fruits—a token of the bringing to God of the whole community's "produce", and, in it, of the whole community itself, and of all creation. These ideas go back to early writers such as Irenaeus and Cyprian, and find famous expression in Augustine;[2] and they have been widely revived in our own day in many churches where the carrying up of bread and wine from the congregation to the sanctuary has been restored to prominence, in addition to the collection of money.

Essentially this use of the offertory as a symbol of the bringing of the worshippers and of all creation to God seems compatible enough with the New Testament, even if it is there not brought into explicit relation to the eucharistic elements. The offering to God of a sacrifice consisting of ourselves, soul and body (Rom. 12: 1), or of our praises and our deeds of loving service to others (Heb. 13: 16, etc.) is explicitly mentioned.

[1] See A. Nairne, *The Epistle to the Hebrews*, 1922, xxxiv.
[2] Iren. *adv. Haer.* iv. xvii. 4–xviii. 6; Cyprian *de op. et el.* xv. Aug. *serm.* 229.

But (as was said earlier), to be true to the New Testament, one needs to avoid any suggestion that such "sacrifices" are imagined as in themselves things of "merit", winning our salvation. They are simply the response of human gratitude to God's initiative in giving Himself up, in Christ, on our behalf. It is God's act—God's self-giving in Christ—which alone has reconciled us to Him (2 Cor. 5: 19, etc.): the rest—whatever *we* can do—is all response. And it is perhaps significant that nowhere in the New Testament (if the exegesis of Heb. 13: 10 ff. above is right) is there any allusion to the Eucharist as in any sense the offering of the sacrifice of Christ—still less are the loaf and the cup called a "sacrifice". They are means, rather, of participating in a sacrifice already achieved once and for all (1 Cor. 10: 16; Heb. 9: 12, etc.). That is to say, in the New Testament the death of Christ is sometimes described as a sacrifice, and so is the offering of praise and obedient service by Christians (albeit in a sense which must evidently be secondary to and dependent on Christ's sacrifice). But the sharing of the bread and wine, in the context of remembrance of that sacrifice and of thanksgiving for it, is looked upon not as a fresh sacrifice but as a uniting of ourselves with Christ in His self-giving, and as a renewal of the obligations and relationships which spring from the once-and-for-all death of Christ (1 Cor. 10: 16–18, 11: 26–34). It seems best, therefore, to describe this not as *offering a sacrifice* but rather as a realistic *entering into and sharing of Christ's sacrifice*.[1]

The second observation concerns the meaning of blessing and thanksgiving. There is no doubt that Jewish ideas and practice strongly influenced the words used over the bread and wine. In the *Didache* (9: 2, etc.) one can actually watch a Christian adaptation of a Jewish formula in progress. The Jewish formula gave thanks for God's "servant"

---

[1] See C. F. D. Moule, *The Sacrifice of Christ*, 1956. If 1 Clem. 44: 4 (the presbyter-episcopi *offering the gifts of their episkope*) is evidence for a sacrificial interpretation within the New Testament period, at any rate it is not within the New Testament canon. Here, among other places, it does *not* present a parallel to Hebrews. E. L. Mascall, in "The Offertory in the Eucharist", *Parish and People* 21, Autumn 1957, 11 ff., is concerned to distinguish the offertory (as only the preparation for sacrifice) from the sacrifice itself; but this (as J. G. Davies shows in "The Meaning of the Offertory", *Parish and People* 22, Spring 1958, 3 ff.) is an arbitrary division. It is better to see the entire action as one and indivisible (and, I would add, even to accept the present position of the prayer of oblation in the 1662 *Book of Common Prayer*). But it is further necessary, as I see it, to distinguish even the whole eucharistic action from the sacrifice itself, if we are to be true to N.T. emphases. But here we are in very deep doctrinal and liturgical water; and much depends upon our definition of sacrifice.

David; the Christian adds, in parallel, a reference to God's "servant" Jesus.[1] But quite apart from any details of wording, the Jewish conception of "benediction" must be given its due weight. J.-P. Audet argues[2] that the Jewish *berakah* or "blessing" is not exactly mere thanksgiving: it is rather an outburst of praise—a jubilant declaration of God's prowess and exploits, both in creation and in history. It is something more wholly God-centred than even the thanking God for specific mercies: it is adoration. There are innumerable examples of this type of adoring praise in the Old Testament and other Jewish literature; and it is the spirit of this, rather than of "mere" thanksgiving, which no doubt largely inspires the Christian formulae, even though (in such a context), they may be indifferently described both by $\epsilon\dot{v}\lambda o\gamma\epsilon\hat{i}\nu$ ("bless") and $\epsilon\dot{v}\chi\alpha\rho\iota\sigma\tau\epsilon\hat{i}\nu$ ("give thanks").[3] Majestic examples of Christian benedictions are to be found in Eph. 1 and 1 Pet. 1, although these are not explicitly connected with sacramental, "eucharistic" worship.

From Jewish antecedents, and still more from the Christian understanding of the Holy Spirit, it follows, moreover, that, strictly speaking, the object of the verbs $\epsilon\dot{v}\lambda o\gamma\epsilon\hat{i}\nu$ and $\epsilon\dot{v}\chi\alpha\rho\iota\sigma\tau\epsilon\hat{i}\nu$ is God Himself, not the materials, bread and wine. Even though, writing (may we not suppose?) rather loosely, St. Paul in 1 Cor. 10: 16 seems to make the cup the object (cf. Luke 9: 16, in the feeding of the multitude, but contrast Mark 6: 41; Matt. 14: 19), it is contrary to the outlook of Judaism and of the New Testament generally to pronounce a blessing (let alone to invoke the Holy Spirit) on impersonal, material objects;[4] and it seems reasonable to believe that St. Paul *means* "the 'cup of blessing' *regarding which* (or *over which*) we bless (God)".[5] At any rate, an "epiclesis", or invocation of the Holy Spirit *upon non-personal objects* is alien to the New Testament doctrine of the Holy Spirit and of persons, and is a retrograde step. Non-personal objects may be conse-

---

[1] See C. F. D. Moule, "The Influence of Circumstances on the use of Christological Terms", *J.T.S.* n.s. X. 2, Oct. 1959, 252.

[2] As in Note 2, p. 22; 377 ff.

[3] As others, e.g. F. Gavin, *The Jewish Antecedents of the Christian Sacraments*, 1928, 71 f., had already pointed out.

[4] 1 Sam. 9: 13 (Samuel blesses the sacrifice) is not a common usage. It is rather different when the "blessing" is conceived of as "making prosperous": Deut. 28: 5 ("blessed shall be thy basket and thy kneadingtrough"), Prov. 5: 18 ("let thy fountain be blessed"). In general, the Hebrew *brk*, "bless", is distinguished from *ḳdš*, "consecrate".

[5] See Jeremias (as in Note 2, p. 15), 119. And note that in Matt. 26: 26 the Old Syriac has "blessed *over it*" where the Greek has simply $\epsilon\dot{v}\lambda o\gamma\dot{\eta}\sigma\alpha s$.

crated, that is, dedicated for a special purpose in the service of God, but not inspired (2 Tim. 3: 16 is exceptional). Incidentally, it is of course true that it is logically redundant to invoke the Spirit even upon persons, when those persons have, as baptized Christians, already received the Spirit. But if "the Lord be with thee!" is a legitimate salutation, one can scarcely quarrel with an invocation of the Spirit in a similar context.[1]

5. The Homily and the Scripture

So far, nothing has been said about scripture-reading or preaching at the Eucharist, and it is safe to assume that, at least in the earliest days, this was not a *sine qua non* of its celebration. But sooner or later this element came in as a regular part of the proceedings, and it claims our attention at this point.

It is a mistake to assume that a eucharistic sermon, when it did occur, was always and necessarily different in kind from a sermon in another context.[2] Accordingly, the topic of homilies or sermons in general will be taken up later, under the heading of "other types of worship". But if, as is intrinsically likely, an apostolic letter sometimes met with its first reading when the community were assembled for eucharistic worship, that in itself testifies to the wide range and the general character of even a eucharistic homily. Of the New Testament epistles, the most noteworthy in this connexion is 1 Corinthians, which, in its closing verses, contains:

(*a*) allusion (possibly) to the "kiss of peace" (16: 20),[3]

(*b*) a "fencing of the table", in the form of a ban upon non-Christians (16: 22),[4]

(*c*) (perhaps) the eucharistic invocation in its Aramaic form, *marana tha*, "Our Lord, come!" (16: 22, but see the discussion below, pp. 70 f.): and finally

(*d*) the grace (16: 23).

All this, it has been pointed out, corresponds with the ejaculations in

---

[1] This question is discussed by J. G. Davies, *The Spirit, the Church, and the Sacraments*, 1954, and by A. R. George, "The Work of the Holy Spirit in the Sacraments", *The London Quarterly and Holborn Review*, 1955, 185 ff., where the epiclesis is also discussed.

[2] *Contra* R. H. Fuller, *What is Liturgical Preaching?*, 1957.

[3] On this, see C. Spicq (as in Note 1, p. 19), 339 f., 340, n.1. J .B. Lightfoot (as Spicq observes) sees no direct allusion to liturgy in the phrase at this date (*Notes on Epistles of St. Paul*, 1895, 90).

[4] See G. Bornkamm (as in Note 2, p. 22).

Didache 10: 6. If this really means that St. Paul actually designed this long epistle with the expectation that it would be read at a worship assembly, just before the Eucharist,[1] then we must suppose that he, at least, saw nothing inappropriate in a eucharistic homily which, as well as eucharistic references, contained exhortation, rebuke, and advice about a whole range of topics, as well as elaborate doctrinal passages. But one is bound to admit that this expressly eucharistic connexion is only conjecture and that there is very little further evidence within the New Testament that such was the regular intention with epistles from pastors or even with St. Paul's in particular; and even the *Didache* formulae occur perplexingly *after*, not *before* the eucharistic prayer (unless, indeed, the prayer in the *Didache* is only a preliminary to the true Eucharist). [2] There is something to be said for dissociating the end of I Corinthians from the Eucharist after all.[3]

All that one can be sure of is that apostolic letters were read at assemblies of Christians (cf. Col. 4: 16; Philem. 2; Rev. 1: 3) when there must at the very least have been prayer of some sort, and there may often have been eucharistic worship; and it is likely enough that, when there was no apostolic message, a homily of a quite general nature may sometimes have been delivered even at a specifically eucharistic gathering.

On the other hand, when the Eucharist was at Passover time, or in so far as the Eucharist was to some extent always paschal, the tendency (other things being equal) would be to relate the eucharistic homily specifically to the Christian paschal theme. The Jewish custom of expounding the meaning of the exodus at Passover time—both on Passover eve and at the paschal meal itself—may very well have provided the model. It has even been suggested that the Gospels themselves as a whole bear the stamp of the Passover *haggadah* or exposition.[4] A

[1] See H. Lietzmann, *Mass and Lord's Supper*, Eng. trans., 1953, p. 186; J. A. T. Robinson, "Traces of a Liturgical Sequence in I Cor. 16: 20–24", *J.T.S.* n.s. IV. 1, April 1953, 38 ff.

[2] See Note 2, p. 22.

[3] Why should not the *maranatha* be an invocation to reinforce the "ban" (*anathema*), rather than a eucharistic invocation? The "come, Lord Jesus!" of Rev. 22: 20 follows a terrific "ban" (*vv.* 18 f.). Even in *Didache* 10: 6 maranatha follows an exclusion phrase, rather than presenting itself as a eucharistic invocation proper. See E. Peterson, *ΕΙΣ ΘΕΟΣ*, 1926, 130 f., C. F. D. Moule, "A Reconsideration of the Context of *Maranatha*", *J.N.T.S.* VI. 3, July 1960, 307 ff.

[4] D. Daube's article as in Note 2, p. 11.

post-New Testament example of a Christian paschal homily may be seen in the very remarkable sermon of Melito.[1]

So much for the eucharistic homily as such. But here a fact must be noted which might otherwise cause confusion, namely that apostolic epistles which we have just been discussing as "homilies" or sermons and which were as yet no part of scripture, today constitute part of the *scripture* readings at the Eucharist. We are used to both readings from scripture *and* (in some Churches) a sermon at the Eucharist. Whether it was the regular practice in the very earliest days (as later; cf. Justin *Apol.* i. 67) to have readings at the Eucharist from the scripture (i.e. from the Old Testament) cannot be said with certainty. We may safely assume that the synagogue practice of reading from the Law and the Prophets must have influenced Jewish Christianity, and probably at the Eucharist as well as on other occasions (1 Tim. 4: 13 is generally interpreted as a reference to the public reading of scripture). But how far, it is not possible to say. One may simply note that, whereas today there may be (*a*) readings from the Old Testament (in some communions, e.g. S. India), from Epistles, and from Gospels and (*b*) a sermon, in those early days of the New Testament period the only scripture available was the Old Testament, while the Epistles and the Gospel traditions were then in the making and were rather in the category of a homily.

Looking back over this review of such evidence as the New Testament affords in respect of eucharistic practice, we must confess that the evidence is slight and vague. What may, however, be said is that it does justify the use of bread and wine, in the context of congregational thanksgiving, and of the words of Christ in the upper room, and of the recollection of His death, as a means of uniting the worshippers with Christ in His death and resurrection: that is, as a sacrament. It is questionable whether originally the breaking of the bread and the pouring of the wine were intended to symbolize the breaking of Christ's body and the shedding of His blood; but it is difficult to avoid the conclusion that, from the first, the bread and wine were being used in direct relation to the death of Christ and to the union of believers with Him in it. Equally clear is the close relationship between the sacramental rite and the ordinary fellowship of the Christian community. To abuse the latter is to do grave despite to the former (1 Cor. 11). The New Testament has no room for religious practices in water-tight compartments.

[1] Ed. Campbell Bonner, 1940.

On the other hand, not *all* of the interpretations of the Eucharist which quite soon begin to appear may be justified by the New Testament. This applies in particular, as has already been observed, to the interpretation of the elements as a *sacrificial* offering in the strict sense, and to the "blessing" (as distinct from "consecrating", that is, dedicating) of the elements.[1]

---

[1] It has been customary, especially since G. Dix (as in Note 1, p. 28), 50, to speak of the fourfold shape of the liturgy as it emerged from the N.T. antecedents. In an article already referred to ("The Meaning of the Offertory", *Parish and People* 22, Spring 1958, 3 ff.) J. G. Davies justly challenges this as an oversimplification.

III

BAPTISM

THE EUCHARIST HAS been discussed first, simply because the account of the early Church's activities in Acts 2: 42 seemed a suitable starting-point and led on to this topic. But in fact it is Baptism which is mentioned first (in *vv.* 38, 41), and throughout the New Testament there is far more frequent reference to Baptism than to Holy Communion. This may be because the Eucharist, for all its great importance in the Church's life, is, in a sense, secondary, as only a reappropriation and renewal of the definitive fact of Baptism. Baptism and Eucharist were very closely connected, adult Baptism no doubt leading, in normal circumstances, straight to the first Eucharist; and, of the two, Baptism was the normative rite. As the primary and decisive step, as the rite of entry into the Church, as *the* summary *par excellence* of the whole action of the Gospel, it naturally dominated and set the pattern for theological thought.[1]

In the New Testament, it is fair to say,[2] Baptism is assumed as the way of entry into the Christian Church. It is taken as a matter of course in (to cite only some of the passages) Acts 2: 38, 41; 8: 13, 16, 36; 9: 18; 10: 47; 19: 3; Rom. 6: 3; 1 Cor. 6: 11 (apparently), 12: 13; Gal. 3: 27; Eph. 4: 5; Col. 2: 12; Tit. 3: 5; Heb. 6: 2 (perhaps), 4 (probably); 1 Pet. 3: 21. And although Matt. 28: 19 is the only New Testament reference to an actual command by Christ to perform it, and although the context of this passage and its trinitarian formula raise serious doubts about its authenticity as a literal *verbum Domini*, yet, even without it, there is little doubt as to the universality of the practice in the Christian Church. In some of the passages just adduced, it is simply assumed that Christians, as such, must have been baptized; and the same is at least implied in others.

Moreover, the whole context of thought attaching to Baptism in the

---

[1] C. F. D. Moule, "The Judgment theme in the Sacraments" (as in Note 1, p. 31), 454 ff.

[2] Though see S. I. Buse in A. Gilmore (ed.), *Christian Baptism*, 1959, 115 ff., for hesitations.

New Testament is clearly enough a reflection of Christ's own ministry:[1] His own baptism, His special endowment by the Spirit, His life of service, His death, His resurrection—this, which is the "pattern" of the Gospel-story, is the "pattern" also of Christian Baptism. It is an epitome of the "Abba! Father!", the cry of obedient sonship, which is the key to the understanding both of Christ's relationship with God and with the Holy Spirit, and of believers' adoption as sons of God through Christ in the power of the Spirit. If this is so, it becomes of less moment to determine the remoter antecedents of Christian Baptism. This, which is undeniably a fascinating subject, must not be pursued here. The discovery of the Dead Sea Scrolls has given a new impetus to this inquiry, and readers are referred to the vast literature which it has evoked.[2]

Actual descriptions of Christian Baptisms in the New Testament are tantalizingly brief. The most circumstantial is that of the Ethiopian in Acts 8, in which, as is well known, the Western text (v. 37) includes a short baptismal creed. St. Paul's baptism is even more briefly described in Acts 9. In Acts 19: 1 ff. there is another short account of the baptism of a particular group of persons. The most perplexing question attaching to the Acts evidence is that of the relation between Baptism and the reception of the Spirit.[3] In the case of the mission of Philip the Evangelist in Samaria (Acts 8) baptism with water precedes the coming of the Spirit, which occurs only later, with the imposition of apostolic hands. In the case of Cornelius and his company (Acts 10) the Spirit anticipates baptism, and that without imposition of hands. In the case of the disciples found by Paul at Ephesus (Acts 19) baptism into the name of Jesus is forthwith followed by imposition of hands with manifestations of the Spirit's presence, the disciples having previously been baptized only with John the Baptist's baptism. The question of the imposition of hands is an obscure one: it is further discussed below (pp. 50, 54). In any case, it is not of primary importance. The controlling consideration is a comparatively simple one: that, however many other religions or groups use water-lustration or comparable water-rites, the Christian water-rite is distinctive in that it is in(to) the Name of Jesus and in-

[1] See W. F. Flemington, *The New Testament Doctrine of Baptism*, 1948, *passim*; D. M. Baillie, *The Theology of the Sacraments*, 1957, 75 ff. Further discussion of this issue is to be found in A. Gilmore (ed.), as in preceding Note, especially R. E. O. White (pp. 84 ff.).

[2] See e.g., J. A. T. Robinson, "The Baptism of John and the Qumran Community", *H.T.R.*, L. 3, 1957, and literature referred to there.

[3] See G. W. H. Lampe, *The Seal of the Spirit*, 1951.

volves reception of the Spirit:[1] whereas John baptized only with water, Christian baptism is distinctively with Spirit also (Matt. 3: 11; John 1: 26, 33; Acts 1: 5; 2: 38). That the temporal relation between the use of water and the manifestation of the Spirit is variable, is not really surprising: normally (in adult conversion) simultaneous, they may be separated in time—and that in either direction—according to circumstances. The same applies to the moment of conscious "decision for Christ". This may precede baptism by days (as in St. Paul's case) or weeks (as was no doubt true of many catechumens as soon as teaching and training became at all systematic),[2] or even years; equally it may be almost simultaneous, as appears to have been the case with the Philippian gaoler (Acts 16: 33) and many other early sudden conversions. Further observations on the order of events will be made later.

When it came to the point of baptism, it was natural that the question should be asked "Is there anything to prevent our taking this step?"—a question akin to that in the story of the Ethiopian (Acts 8: 36 —though "What is there to prevent . . . ?" is not quite the same): so natural that one hesitates to see in it, with Cullmann,[3] a technical term of the baptismal "scrutinies", still less to link it with the Gospel narrative about the disciples attempting to prevent children approaching Jesus (Mark 10: 14, etc.).

As for the thorny question of the baptism of infants and children, the following observations may be offered. First, there is no doubt that any Jewish Christian community, familiar with circumcision in infancy (outside Judaism, the circumcision of infants seems to be rare),[4] would have a natural predisposition in favour of *some* infancy rite. Against this, however, it has to be admitted that the only close analogy in orthodox Judaism to the Christian *water*-rite was, by definition, an *adult* one, namely proselyte baptism; and moreover, that since circumcision was only for males, it is hardly likely to have been the most influential of analogies for the Christian rite of entry, which was for both sexes.[5] If, on the other hand, one urges that 1 Cor. 7: 14 indicates

[1] Despite A. Gilmore (as in Note 2, p. 42), 115.

[2] When was the catechumenate established? Heb. 6: 1 f. seems to be a hint. For the curious order "*kerygma*", baptism, "*didache*", see J.-P. Audet (as in Note 2, p. 22), 359.

[3] *Baptism in the New Testament*, Eng. trans., 1950, Appendix 71 ff. For criticism, see A. Gilmore, 125.

[4] See A. Gilmore, 56, n. 4.

[5] See H. H. Rowley, cited by A. Gilmore, 24, and *E.T.* LXIV, 1952–3, 362; LXV, 1953–4, 158; D. Daube (as in Note 2, p. 27), 106, 113.

that St. Paul was ready to entertain a conception of the "hallowing" or sanctification of the unwitting child by the dedication of a parent, nevertheless this same context (it has been justly observed)[1] alludes equally to the hallowing of an adult non-Christian partner, and does not, therefore, take us any way towards a doctrine of entry into the Christian Church by proxy. The allusion to baptism on behalf of the dead (1 Cor. 15: 29) might be more to the point; but it is too obscure to carry much weight.[2]

Thus, so far as hints as to theory go, or analogies to practice, the upshot is not entirely clear, although on the whole adult baptism has, thus far at least, the better of the argument.

As for the actual practice by Christians of infant baptism, there is no direct evidence for it in the New Testament. The baptism of entire households (as of the Philippian gaoler, Acts 16: 33) may be intended to include infants, but it is impossible to prove it. That Jesus *blessed* little children (Mark 10: 13–16) has nothing directly to do with the matter. If paedobaptism, therefore, is to be justified, it must be on other grounds than that of evidence for the practice within the New Testament. What is clear is that, in any case, if and when infant baptism is practised, it cannot by itself carry the whole of the theological implications of adult baptism. Any infant-rite necessarily implies some further step at years of discretion. The reference in Acts 8: 15–17 to the imposition of apostolic hands at some interval after baptism provides a convenient Biblical precedent for the use of the imposition of episcopal hands at what is now called Confirmation. But, if so, it has to be added that Acts 19: 5 f. makes it clear that the imposition of hands was integral to the baptism; and on any showing the use of the water and the receiving of the Spirit belong *theologically* together, whether or not there is a visible focus of the latter at some remove (chronologically speaking) from the former. (See further Heb. 6: 2.) In short, Baptism, what is now called "Confirmation", and Eucharist form together a single complex of entry into the Christian Church.[3]

But for our present purpose what is important is the nature of the worship and procedures associated with Baptism. For this the direct

---

[1] A. Gilmore (ed.), as in Note 2, p. 42, 148.

[2] Cf. J. Jeremias in *J.N.T.S.* II. 3, Feb. 1956, 155 f. See M. Raeder "Vikariatstaufe in 1 Cor. 15^{29}?" *Z.N.T.W.* XLVI, 1955, 258 ff. for an unusual theory (viz. that the phrase means "those who are baptized with a view to being united, at the resurrection, with their Christian friends who have died").

[3] G. W. H. Lampe, as in Note 3, p. 43, *passim*.

evidence within the New Testament is meagre. It scarcely goes beyond the use of the name of Jesus, preceded by some brief confession of faith, doubtless given in answer to interrogation, as virtually in the Western text of Acts 8: 37: "Philip said, 'If you believe with your whole heart, it is possible'. And in reply he said, 'I believe that Jesus Christ is the Son of God'." It is possible that the candidate's declaration of loyalty, if not his profession of faith, is alluded to in the notoriously obscure word ἐπερώτημα in 1 Pet. 3: 21. But the debate on its meaning still continues.[1]

The nature of the baptismal creed has been matter for prolonged discussion. The rudimentary one just quoted is Christological, not theological, still less trinitarian; and apart from Matt. 28: 19 there is no direct evidence in the New Testament for a trinitarian formula in the administration of Baptism (and indeed even Matt. 28: 19 is not strictly to be so described).[2] It has, indeed, been argued by O. Cullmann[3] that the earliest creeds were thus simply confessions of faith in Jesus as Lord; that the clauses relating to belief in God the Father were added when pagans, with no monotheistic background, were brought in; and that the clauses about the Spirit grew from the association of the Holy Spirit with Baptism. This has been criticized (e.g. by J. N. D. Kelly);[4] but the truth may well be that different practices in this regard were indeed evoked by different circumstances. As G. F. Moore had suggested long before, it may be that, whereas within Judaism the "theological", monotheistic confession could be taken for granted, in the pagan world a fuller creed may have been necessary from the earliest times.[5] Obviously, in the last analysis, a Christology is itself impossible without the confession of God as Creator and as the Father of our Lord Jesus Christ.

But if there is only scanty direct evidence for the words used at Baptism, beyond a minimal credal formula, or for the procedure, beyond the use of water and, sometimes at least, the imposition of hands, the New Testament contains many allusions to the meaning of Baptism, and from these it is possible to reconstruct rather more fully what may have been said and done at adult baptisms.

Perhaps after fasting (cf. Acts 9: 9, 19; 13: 2 f.), and after it had been

[1] See I. Buse in A. Gilmore (ed.), as in Note 2, p. 42, 175
[2] Cf. J.-P. Audet, as in Note 2, p. 22, 362 f. `
[3] *The Earliest Christian Confessions*, Eng. trans., 1949.
[4] *Early Christian Creeds*, 1950, 25 ff.
[5] *Judaism* I, 1927, 188 f.

established by question and answer that the candidate was suitable and ready, there was, first, the renunciation of the whole kingdom of evil and of the whole self as attached to that realm. It is possible that already (as in later days) this was symbolized by the candidate facing westwards for the renunciation; and it may have been associated also with the act of removing the clothes preparatory to going into the water. Certainly St. Paul speaks of the death of Christ Himself, and of the Christian with Christ, as divestiture (see Col. 2: 11, 15; 3: 9; cf. Rom. 13: 12; Eph. 4: 22; Jas. 1: 21; 1 Pet. 2: 1); and he describes Christians as being clothed with Christ (Gal. 3: 27, cf. Rom. 13: 14), or with "the new humanity" (Eph. 4: 24; Col. 3: 10); and it is difficult not to associate this metaphor with the actual movements of the baptized.

In parenthesis, it may be remarked here (returning for a moment to the analogy of circumcision) that this "stripping off" of the old life, the old self, the whole world of the old life, was also comparable, in a way, to circumcision; for whereas circumcision was a symbolic "divestiture" of a small part of the body which might be taken to represent impurity and evil, Baptism involved a divestiture or stripping off of the entire self; and it went back to the moment when Christ surrendered and "stripped off" His own body. The comparison with circumcision is worked out in Col. 2: 11 f.

Next came, presumably, the formal declaration of faith, the creed, the candidate perhaps facing east; then the water. The Ethiopian in Acts 8: 38 "went down" into the water with Philip the evangelist; and John the Baptist doubtless caused his converts actually to wade into the Jordan. Whether the baptizand was then actually plunged beneath the surface or whether, as he stood in the water, he poured the water over himself, or had it poured over him, does not appear from the New Testament itself. All that can be said is that total immersion would fit well with the doctrine of death and burial with Christ and with the symbolism of the drowning of wickedness as in the Deluge. On the other hand, it must be noted that the verb $\beta\alpha\pi\tau\iota\zeta\epsilon\iota\nu$ and the noun $\beta\alpha\pi\tau\iota\sigma\mu\alpha$ are not exact equivalents of $\beta\alpha\pi\tau\epsilon\iota\nu$ and $\beta\alpha\phi\eta$ respectively. The latter mean "to dip" and "dipping"; but $\beta\alpha\pi\tau\iota\zeta\epsilon\iota\nu$ means "to deluge" or "douse", and so far no occurrence of $\beta\alpha\pi\tau\iota\sigma\mu\alpha$ is known except in its technical sense of "baptism". It looks, therefore, as though Baptism was properly neither a mere sprinkling ($\dot{\rho}\alpha\nu\tau\iota\sigma\mu\dot{o}\varsigma$) nor an immersing ($\beta\alpha\phi\eta$), but a "deluging" with water.[1] Later times, as we

[1] D. W. B. Robinson, *The Meaning of Baptism*, 1958, 6 ff., and *T.W.N.T. s.v.*

know, presented a variety of practice—immersing, sprinkling, pouring (cf. *Didache* 7).

Further, there is, in the New Testament, no direct evidence for the exact relation of the baptismal formula to the use of the water. We are only told that Baptism was in or into the name of (the Lord) Jesus— that is, the name was uttered (whether by the officiant or by the candidate or by both),[1] and also Baptism was *into* the name, that is, the ownership, the protection of Jesus, and into membership in Him.[2] Still less is there evidence of any symbolic connexion of the formula of Baptism with the actual movements in the use of the water (as, for instance, there was sooner or later a triple immersion or sprinkling to match the trinitarian formula). The nearest we come to any explicit connexion between the formula and the water is in the phrase in Eph. 5: 26, where Christ is spoken of as cleansing his Bride the Church "in the bath of water in utterance" ($\dot{\epsilon}\nu$ $\dot{\rho}\dot{\eta}\mu\alpha\tau\iota$). The precise meaning of the last two words is much debated. P. Bonnard, commenting on the passage,[3] and drawing upon S. Hanson's *The Unity of the Church in the New Testament. Colossians and Ephesians* (Upsala, 1946), thinks that the reference is neither to the whole Gospel (as purifying the Church simultaneously with baptism), nor merely to the baptismal formula itself, but rather, in a more general way, to the utterance which plays its part in the celebration of baptism whether on the lips of the officiant or of the baptizand himself. Professor E. C. Ratcliff[4] suggests, more plausibly, that the "utterance" is the Lord's own address to His Bride. In the early Syrian baptismal rite, the ministrant actually said "Thou art my Son, this day have I begotten thee."

Coming up, or out, from the water, the newly baptized would then be re-clothed—an action which might symbolize the "putting on" of the risen Christ, the being clothed with the new humanity, with the Body of Christ. It is the correlative action to the divestiture of the old. Sooner or later it seems to have been made a formal symbol, by the use of a special garment.[5]

---

[1] See J. H. Crehan, *Early Christian Baptism and the Creed*, 1950.

[2] See bibliography in A. Gilmore (ed.), as in Note 2, p. 42, 122, and add W. Heitmüller, *Im Namen Jesu*, 1903.

[3] In *Commentaire du Nouveau Testament*, 1953.

[4] In a private communication. See *Didascalia Apostolorum. The Syriac Version translated and accompanied by the Verona Latin Fragments, with an Introduction and Notes*, R. Hugh Connolly, 1929, 93.

[5] See F. L. Cross (ed.), *The Oxford Dictionary of the Christian Church*, 1957, *s.v.* Chrysom.

This may have been followed, as in St. Paul's case (Acts 9: 19), by the breaking of a previous fast; and the food might symbolize the entry of the chosen People into the Promised Land. Just as the Israelites, on their first entry into Palestine, "ate of the fruit of the land of Canaan that year" (Josh. 5: 12), so Christians are described in Heb. 6: 4 f. as having "tasted" the heavenly gift and the word of God and the powers of the coming age (cf. Ps. 34: 8 and 1 Pet. 2: 3), metaphors which would certainly gain in point if a ritual breaking of the fast was customary at Baptism. Sooner or later honey was a recognized food on this occasion (cf. Luke 24: 42, *v. l.*, *Tert. de cor. mil.*, 3, Hippolytus, *Ap. Trad.* xxiii. 2, and, incidentally, *Joseph and Aseneth*—editions as in Note 4, p. 22 and 3, p. 23). The standing description of the Promised Land in the Old Testament is of a land flowing with *milk*, as well as honey; but in the New Testament milk seems to be a metaphor chiefly for the food of the immature (whether commendably, as in 1 Pet. 2: 2, or, in a context of rebuke for retarded growth, in 1 Cor. 3: 2).

But we must return now to a vital question already alluded to earlier—the relation between Baptism and the Holy Spirit. That the two belong theologically together is clear enough from such passages as Acts 10: 45–47; 19: 1–6; 1 Cor. 12: 13; and accordingly it seems right in Tit. 3: 5 to translate " . . . he saved us through the bath of regeneration *and of* renewal by the Holy Spirit", rather than ". . . through the bath of regeneration *and through* renewal . . ." (as though these were two separable "moments").[1]

But if so, was there in New Testament times a visible "focus" of the reception of the Spirit at Baptism? Later at any rate "chrismation", that is, symbolic anointing with oil, was used, and (or) the imposition of hands. We have already looked at references to the imposition of hands (pp. 48, 50 above). It is impossible to be certain whether this was regular practice at, or after, Baptism: only that it was practised at least sometimes. Still less can be said with certainty of chrismation. In 1 John 2: 20 ff. reference is made to a "chrism" possessed by Christians. This is clearly a metaphorical reference either to the reception of the Spirit or to the possession of the Gospel—that "knowledge" through which the Spirit is received.[2] But whether the use of the metaphor implies the use of material chrism at Baptism is another matter. It is quite possible, though not demonstrable, that it does. It is known that

---

[1] G. W. H. Lampe (as in Note 3, p. 43), 59 f.
[2] See C. H. Dodd, Moffatt Commentary, 1946, *in loc.*

in a later period chrismation in some uses preceded and in others followed Baptism, and it is just possible that in 1 John 5: 8 the order "Spirit, water, and blood" may reflect the particular usage of the churches of the Johannine circle—chrism first, then Baptism, then Eucharist.[1] But the order need not be significant; for if "water and blood" were already linked together by the Johannine Passion narrative (John 19: 34 f.) it is difficult to see how the mention of the Spirit could be inserted between the two. Again, in 2 Cor. 1: 21 Christians are spoken of as "anointed" by God; but it is impossible to say whether this is derived from an actual rite, or is not rather a metaphorical description of the status of Christians as adopted into the community of "Christ", the "Messiah", the "Anointed".

The same problem attaches to the metaphor of sealing ($\sigma\phi\rho\alpha\gamma\iota\zeta\epsilon\iota\nu$). In the same context as the passage just cited, namely in 2 Cor. 1: 22, Christians are also described as "sealed" by God; and this word is applied twice in Ephesians (1: 13; 4: 30), and that with reference to the reception of the Spirit. Moreover, in an obscure passage, 2 Tim. 2: 19, God's "foundation" is described as bearing as its "seal" the phrase "the Lord knows those who are his". Since there is a long Old Testament and Jewish history to this metaphor, including the idea that God's redeemed are marked with a distinguishing sign (the *taw* or cross), and that circumcision is a "seal", it appears that the word is closely associated with rites denoting "belonging" to God, and is thus highly appropriate to a rite of entry into a religious community.[2] But, once more, it would be running ahead of the evidence to deduce, simply from the New Testament use of the word, that already the sign of the cross was actually made at Baptism. It may well be so; but we cannot be certain.

A further term evidently associated with Baptism was enlightenment. In certain pagan mystery initiations, a part was played by a brilliantly illuminated room into which the initiate was suddenly introduced after being kept in darkness. And in Christian Baptism a lighted taper was sooner or later being used as a symbol. But there is nothing in the New Testament to suggest that there was as yet in the Christian rite of entry any literal symbol corresponding to the metaphors of

[1] See T. W. Manson, "Entry into Membership of the Early Church", *J.T.S.* XLVIII, 1947, 25 ff.; W. Nauck, *Die Tradition und der Charakter des ersten Johannes-briefes*, 1957, 147 ff.; A. Gilmore (ed.), as in Note 2, p. 42, 167 ff.

[2] See bibliography in E. Dinkler, "Jesu Wort vom Kreuztragen" in *Neutestamentliche Studien für Bultmann*, 1954, 117.

enlightenment; and the use in Heb. 6: 4 of the participle "enlightened" (φωτισθέντες), in what, as has already been mentioned, is almost certainly a baptismal context, is intelligible enough as a vivid but metaphorical allusion to the spiritual condition of those whom God has called "out of darkness into his marvellous light" (1 Pet. 2: 9). It is possible that the little snatch of Christian hymnody (for such it seems to be) in Eph. 5: 14 belonged originally to a baptismal setting:

> Awake, sleeper, and arise from among the dead!
> and Christ shall shine upon you;

but again, the metaphor need not imply ritual. By the time of Justin "enlightenment", φωτισμός, has become a technical term simply for Baptism.[1]

This, then, is the broad pattern made up of the different parts of entry into the Christian Church—this sacramental sharing in the death and life of Christ—indicated or hinted at by our evidence: renunciation, penitence, fasting, divestiture; confession of faith; Baptism in the name of the Lord Jesus; clothing, anointing, imposition of hands, tasting the new food. And the "tasting" might well be identical with the first Eucharist, which added the coping stone to the whole structure of entry into the Church. But two further conceptions closely attaching to this death and new life still require mention, namely rebirth and cleansing.

"Rebirth" or "rebegetting", so far as the New Testament goes, is confined to John 3: 3 ff. and 1 Pet. 1: 3, 23 (cf. 2: 2). But "regeneration", a closely allied metaphor, occurs in Tit. 3: 5; and "giving birth", simply, in Jas. 1: 18 (curiously, with *God* as the subject of this female metaphor); and although St. Paul does not use just these words, his "new creation" (2 Cor. 5: 17; Gal. 6: 15), and "new life" (Rom. 6: 4) contain much that overlaps these same ideas; and in 1 Cor. 4: 15 he says that through the Gospel he "begot" his converts. Again, only in John 3: 5; Tit. 3: 5 is "water" or the "bath" (and thus, no doubt, Baptism) brought expressly into connexion with any of these terms. But since all these allusions describe, in one way or another, the Christian's new life, they necessarily coincide with the rite of entry into it. On the whole, it is probably a mistake to imagine that the term "new creation" is meant to be limited to the one individual in question; for, being reborn or begotten anew, he finds himself not only renewed individually but possessed of a new world of existence: "when a person comes to be

---

[1] *Apology* i. 61.

united with Christ, there is a new creation" (so 2 Cor. 5: 17 may be interpreted, cf. Gal. 6: 15); his union with Christ in His death introduces him into a new realm of life (Rom. 6: 3 ff.). To be in the new Adam is to walk in Paradise regained: or, more realistically, at least to have had a taste of the age to come (cf. Heb. 6: 5), and to "put on the new humanity" (Eph. 4: 24; Col. 3: 10) is not only to acquire, individually, a reformed character, but to become incorporated in a new "race" of mankind.

Washing or cleansing is, perhaps, the most obvious of all meanings to be attached to a water-ritual. But in fact Baptism is so much more drastic than this and so much more far-reaching in its consequences, that the New Testament only seldom uses this metaphor. Baptism is essentially *death* and *burial*—not mere *washing*. Even in 1 Pet. 3: 20 ff. where the water-motif is at its most prominent, the chief analogy is not in the water that washes (though that may be hinted at in *v.* 21) but in the flood that drowns. As the sinful generation of Noah was drowned, so the sinful self of the baptizand is dead and done with, while his obedient self is rescued and brought, like Noah, safely through water. The Pauline epistles and 1 Peter are at one in this: Baptism is not merely turning over a new leaf—it is death and resurrection.

Only in 1 Cor. 6:11; Eph. 5: 26; Tit. 3:5 and 2 Pet. 1:9 (apart from 1 Pet. 3: 21) is washing fairly clearly implied or stated as a baptismal event. One may perhaps add Rev. 7: 14 (cf. 1: 5, *v. l.*), though the "baptism" in this case was the drastic one of martyrdom.

The relative strength of these two concepts—new birth or new creation after death, and washing after defilement—is of doctrinal moment. As soon as Baptism is treated as *chiefly* a cleansing, the tendency is to interpret it as a cleansing from *past* sins, with the corollary that thereafter the baptized must keep himself clean. But as long as membership in Christ is treated as a new life—as the bringing of a person through death into a new relationship and an entirely new world of existence— the supernatural, wholly divine agency is more prominent. The "indicative", the statement, that we have died and been buried with Christ and are now alive in Him, is a more potent one than the statement that we were once washed. "Become what you are!" is a more deeply Christian imperative than "Keep yourself clean!"[1]

Over and above the evidence thus far reviewed, there are passages in the New Testament where the language of catechetical instructions

[1] Cf. R. Bultmann, "Ignatius und Paulus", in *Studia Paulina* (*in hon.* J. de Zwaan, ed. J. N. Sevenster and W. C. van Unnik, 1953).

to baptizands, and of the baptismal liturgy itself, has, with more or less plausibility, been detected.

In the first place, A. Seeberg long ago, and, more recently, P. Carrington, A. M. Hunter, and E. G. Selwyn[1] have made a good case for the view that much of the ethical instruction which occurs in the Pauline epistles, in 1 Peter, and in James, is a reflection of a fairly constant pattern of instruction given to inquirers. Carrington labelled each section of this instruction with a heading or a catch-word, and the listing of these shows how much of this instruction runs through the New Testament.

Further, it has become fashionable to find in 1 Peter (or within it) a baptismal homily[2] or even an entire liturgy. This latter suggestion, made by H. Preisker, was taken a step further by F. L. Cross [3] who wished to see not merely *a* baptismal liturgy but *the* great Paschal baptismal liturgy of Rome—possibly in St. Peter's own time. No one can doubt that the themes of 1 Peter are wholly appropriate to Baptism. But it is another matter to find here the actual order and wording of the baptismal Eucharist—let alone to detect the very point at which the baptism itself took place. Is it not far more likely an exhortation to those who are suffering, or are threatened with, persecution[4]—an exhortation in the form of a recall to all that their baptism had meant?

The suggestion has been made (as has already been said) that in Eph. 5: 14 we can catch the tones of an ancient baptismal hymn.[5] Perhaps the same may be said of 1 Tim. 3: 16, for this is a poetical form

---

[1] A. Seeberg, *Der Katechismus der Urchristenheit*, 1903; P. Carrington, *The Primitive Christian Catechism*, 1940; A. M. Hunter, *Paul and his Predecessors*, 1940; E. G. Selwyn, *The First Epistle of Peter*, 1946.

[2] See, e.g., B. H. Streeter, *The Primitive Church*, 1929, 115 ff.; and commentaries, e.g. F. W. Beare's, 2nd ed. 1958.

[3] See H. Windisch, *Die Katholischen Briefe*,[3] revised by H. Preisker (Lietzmann, *Handbuch zum N.T.*, 1951); F. L. Cross, *1 Peter: a Paschal Liturgy*, 1954; M. E. Boismard, "Une Liturgie baptismale dans la *Prima Petri*. I. Son influence sur Tit., I Jo.et Col.", *R.B.* 63. 2, April 1956, 182 ff.; "II. Son influence sur l'épître de Jacques", *R.B.* 64. 2, April 1957, 161 ff.

[4] So J. H. A. Hart, in his commentary in *The Expositor's Greek Testament*, 1910, and C. F. D. Moule, "The Nature and Purpose of 1 Peter", *J.N.T.S.* III. 1, Nov. 1956, 1 ff. I owe an apology for having forgotten when writing that paper that Hart had anticipated me in the substance of my theory. See F. W. Beare, as in Note 2 above.

[5] See authorities ancient and modern cited by T. K. Abbott (I.C.C.*n.d.*) *in loc.*; and, more recently, M. Dibelius (Lietzmann, *Handbuch zum N.T.*, 1927), *in loc.*

of a creed, and credal poetry was in place at the baptismal confession.[1]
This is, incidentally, a reminder that, while there were creeds or early
confessions in prose (like Acts 8: 37 in the Western text), there might
equally be hymnic forms: we still use the Apostles' or Nicene Creed
side by side with that poetical creed the *Te Deum*: the one a statement,
the other an adoration and a prayer.[2]

Was Baptism always unrepeatable and administered once for all?
This is generally assumed. Of Christian Baptism it is assumed partly
because St. Paul so obviously treats it as unrepeatable. St. Paul writes
of it as something so closely comparable to one's own death and burial,
and so closely linked with Christ's death and burial, that any going
back on it or repetition of it would have been unthinkable. Baptism is
thus so closely linked with the great "objective" *datum* of Christian
faith—the death of Christ once and for all, the act which, crowning
Christ's own baptism, was the baptism of all mankind—that it becomes
theologically unrepeatable. For Christ (and therefore for the world
collectively) it is *done* and it is *finished*; thereafter, it is for each individual
to apprehend it for himself individually and once. ". . . Christian
baptism is none other than the great baptism of Christ now made
individually effective."[3] Any renewal that there may be will be by some
other, some repetitive rite, the most obvious being the Eucharist. Or
again, it may be put in simple terms of entry: once one has entered a
room one is in; one cannot enter it again without first going back on
what has been done. And if Baptism is the rite of entry into membership of God's Israel, one can no more repeat it than repeatedly be
circumcised.

But the fact that Baptism came, by its theological implications, to be
the sacrament of finality, does not necessarily mean that it was originally, or everywhere, at first so limited. Water-rites in general appear to
be repeatable—for instance in the Qumran sect, and in Judaism generally. If a proselyte was received once and for all by a "baptismal" bath
as well as by circumcision, that did not prevent him from being sub-
sequently "washed" by ritual lustrations again and again. Indeed, whenever Baptism is conceived of primarily as "cleansing", it is not sur-

[1] See commentators *in loc.*

[2] Cf. H. A. Blair, *A Creed Before the Creeds*, 1955, 2 ff.; and for the *Te Deum* as
itself the reflection of the Paschal Liturgy, see E. Kähler, *Studien zum Te Deum
und zur Geschichte des 24 Psalms in der Alten Kirche*, 1958.

[3] J. A. T. Robinson, "The One Baptism as a Category of New Testament
Soteriology", *S.J.T.*6. 3, Sept. 1953, 267; cf. W. Nauck (as in Note 1, p. 50), 179.

prising if it seems to differ only in degree from the subsequent, repeated washing-rites which many branches of Christianity itself employ—sprinkling rituals such as "holy water" at the church door, or the sprinkling of ministrants and congregation at the *Asperges me* . . . (the phrase is from Ps. 51). And it may be that, in certain quarters and in early days, the primary great Baptism of initiation may have been so closely resembled by subsequent lesser lustrations that it may have been difficult to make a clear-cut distinction between the "great" Baptism of initiation and "lesser" baptisms of renewal. The Epistle to the Hebrews (6: 2) alludes to βαπτισμοί in the plural, and (10: 22) recognizes lustrations, although the writer is emphatic (6: 4, cf. 10: 26) about the unrepeatability of Baptism. There is nothing to prove that water-rites were not used in connexion with repentance from what 1 John 5 calls sins not unto death.[1]

However, this is speculation, and in any case applies, if at all, only to the very early days of the Christian Church (except for heretical sects who practised frequent lustrations). If not from the first, then at least very soon, Baptism was the unrepeatable rite of entry, the door into the Church which could be passed through only once; and so the problem of post-baptismal sin arose. The intensity of this problem and the depth of the answers to it vary according to the theory of what Baptism is—a new creation, or a mere cleansing. This is, however, not the place to pursue this matter.[2] Two observations only need be made: first, that, within the New Testament, John 13: 10 is much debated in this connexion, and 1 John 5: 16 ff. is relevant. And second, that, whereas most modern Christian congregations are familiar with the confession of sins as an oft-repeated factor in public worship, it is by no means clear that this was so in New Testament worship.[3]

[1] See M. Black, "The Gospels and the Scrolls", in *Studia Evangelica*(ed. K. Aland, F. L. Cross, J. Daniélou, H. Riesenfeld, W. C. van Unnik, 1959), 568 f.
[2] See W. Telfer, *The Forgiveness of Sins*, 1959.
[3] See E. Schweizer, "Worship, etc." (as in Note 2, p. 31), 203.

IV

OTHER TYPES OF WORSHIP

WAS THERE, IN New Testament times, any distinctively Christian corporate worship other than the sacramental—the baptismal and eucharistic? It is possible, of course, to turn the question by urging that all Christian worship is, as such, sacramental: in the larger sense, the "element" is the congregation assembling and the Gospel being preached (or the celebration of Baptism or the Lord's Supper); the gift of God's grace is Christ who gives Himself and draws the worshippers into His death and resurrection.[1] But if, when asking the question, one abides by the narrower and more usual sense of "sacramental"—the one which has been used hitherto in this inquiry—what is the answer? The answer "yes" is at least as old as Tertullian; *"aut sacrificium"*—note the sacrificial terminology by this time in use; contrast p. 41—*"offertur, aut Dei verbum administratur", de cult fem.* II. xi (*P.L.* I. 144)[2], and it seems so obvious and natural that it would scarcely require discussion had not the opposite opinion been advanced.[3]

Purely *a priori* it seems highly probable that Christians sometimes met and worshipped without any distinctively sacramental activity (in the more specific sense) taking place. It may, admittedly, be a mistake to allege, as it was at one time fashionable to allege, that the Temple and the Synagogue respectively had their counterparts in Christian worship, the Temple in the Sacraments, the Synagogue in the non-sacramental—the two respectively standing for the "Sacraments" and the "Word" of the now familiar Christian terminology. Indeed, nothing has become clearer in recent liturgical revivals than that Sacraments, at any rate, ought not to be isolated or divorced from preaching. But if the Sacraments are in their very nature "evangelic", as embodiments of the whole Gospel, and therefore are necessarily an occasion

---

[1] W. Hahn, *Gottesdienst und Opfer Christi: eine Untersuchung über das Heilsgeschehen im christlichen Gottesdienst,* 1951.

[2] Cited by C. W. Dugmore (as in Note 1, p. 5), 43, n. 2, comparing I Clem. xl.

[3] O. Cullmann, as in Note 1, p. 21. *Contra* E. Schweizer, "Worship, etc.", as in Note 2, p. 31.

for the explicit proclamation and explanation of the Gospel, it does not necessarily follow that the converse is true. We know perfectly well that it is possible to preach and worship effectively—that is, with the manifest blessing of God—on occasions when no Sacrament is actually celebrated at the time. Matins and Evensong are not *ipso facto* a decline from the grace of the primitive Church, provided, of course, that those who so worship also worship "sacramentally" at other times. But, more than that, it is difficult to think of any really alive eucharistic congregation in which there are not "cells"—little groups of friends—who meet from time to time for the more intimate worship of informal Bible study and extempore prayer. It is possible, and indeed convincing, to argue that in such cases the sacramental and the non-sacramental still belong together and are essentially one. That is obviously true. But the fact remains that they are in these cases not coincident in time, and that there *are* meetings for Christian worship which, however closely linked to the public eucharistic assembly, are not at the time sacramental.[1]

Is there any reason to doubt that such meetings took place in the New Testament period? There is certainly nothing to prove that the worship described in 1 Cor. 14 was specifically eucharistic. It is fantastic to argue that because εὐχαριστία (i.e. "thanksgiving") and the *Amen* are mentioned (*vv.* 16 ff.), it must have been eucharistic. Was there ever a Protestant prayer-meeting of the most extempore, non-liturgical type in which thanksgiving and Amens (in profusion) did not occur? According to 1 Cor. 14, on such occasions as these, with which St. Paul was evidently perfectly familiar, members coming to the meeting found various items to contribute (it is worth while to notice how far removed this sort of gathering was from most modern types of worship with a single leader and the rest comparatively passive):[2] one had a psalm to sing, another some instruction to offer; another would suddenly ejaculate an ecstatic utterance in that strange form known as "speaking with tongues"—*glossolalia*, the use of inarticulate cries (as appears from this passage) or of an unknown language (if Acts 2 is taken literally). Mercifully, there might also be forthcoming, from the same person or from another, an interpretation of the practical meaning of this type of ejaculation. Or again, someone might suddenly get up to offer what he or she believed was a revelation given by inspiration, sent by the Holy Spirit to be shared with the other worshippers.

[1] See W. Hahn (as in Note 1, p. 56), 35.
[2] Cf. E. Schweizer, "Worship, etc.", as in Note 2, p. 31.

But in all this there is no mention of any expressly sacramental ingredient.

That the proceedings were anything but sedate is not the point. There was indeed chaotic informality, and St. Paul is concerned to urge that true prophets are ready to yield place to other true prophets (instead of all speaking at once and trying to shout one another down), and that everything must be conducted in an orderly way, since God Himself is the Creator who brought cosmos out of chaos.[1] But there was informality also at eucharistic assemblies, sinking, at its lowest, to sheer disorder and gluttony, or worse. I Cor. 11 is evidence enough for that. The point is merely that there is no evidence that what is described in I Cor. 14 was "eucharistic", or for insisting that every Christian meeting for worship contained an expressly sacramental element. The non-sacramental meeting for thanksgiving and for prayer, for Bible study and mutual edification must have been as natural and as common then as now. Even the sombre and solemn meeting for the excommunication of a sinful member, alluded to in I Cor. 5: 4 f., cannot be simply assumed to have been a strictly sacramental gathering.[2]

Along these lines, again, we must not assume that other instances of the sudden access of the "prophetic" spirit of second sight are necessarily to be associated with sacramental assemblies. There is absolutely nothing to prove that Agabus's prophecies of the impending famine (Acts 11: 28) and of St. Paul's arrest (Acts 21: 10 f.) took place in the context of any worship at all—let alone sacramental worship. On the other hand, in Acts 13: 2 an inspired utterance (attributed directly to the Holy Spirit) is expressly described as having taken place during divine service (whether sacramental or not is another matter) and a period of fasting. The very horrifying utterance "Anathema Jesus!" is

---

[1] An interesting pagan parallel is the function of the "vergers" ($\dot{\rho}\alpha\beta\delta o\hat{v}\chi o\iota$) in the mysteries of Andania, which was to secure that everything be done in a decent and orderly way ($\epsilon\dot{v}\sigma\chi\eta\mu\acute{o}\nu\omega\varsigma$ $\kappa\alpha\grave{\iota}$ $\epsilon\dot{v}\tau\acute{a}\kappa\tau\omega\varsigma$), I.G. V. I, 1390 § 10, cited by R. Bultmann (as in Note 3, p. 17), 461.

[2] The verb $\sigma\upsilon\nu\acute{a}\gamma\omega$ is used in I Cor. 5: 4, and, although it is here clearly not used technically, the corresponding noun, $\sigma\acute{u}\nu\alpha\xi\iota\varsigma$, later came to be a technical term for "the non-Eucharistic 'general meeting' of the whole local church"; G. Dix (as in Note I, p. 28), 18. In passing, why did the words $\sigma\acute{u}\nu\alpha\xi\iota\varsigma$ and $\sigma\upsilon\nu\acute{\epsilon}\lambda\epsilon\upsilon\sigma\iota\varsigma$ become the usual Christian terms, rather than the common word $\sigma\acute{u}\nu o\delta o\varsigma$? The latter occurs, significantly, in the interesting allusions to the worship of "God most high" by a religious fraternity in the first century B.C.: H.T.R. XXIX, 1936, 39 ff.

alluded to in 1 Cor. 12: 3 as though it were a cry which might actually break out suddenly at an assembly where inspired ejaculations were being made, but, again, the type of assembly is not indicated.

Clearly two things are, in all this, of sovereign importance. One is the principle that all the worship, whether formal or informal, whether sacramental or not, should be (to use a fine phrase of Professor W. C. van Unnik's)[1] "in the magnetic field of the Holy Spirit". It is the one Spirit who is, in all, the source of all the varied gifts (1 Cor. 12: 4); it is "in the Holy Spirit" that all prayer is offered (Jude 20). The other matter of importance is that the assembled congregation are deeply responsible for all that occurs. It is with them that rests the vital task of discriminating what is genuine from what is false; they have to find out what God is saying to the Church collectively; they are the check on the individual's inspiration (1 Cor. 14: 29). So shocking a cry as "Anathema Jesus!" is manifestly daemonic, not divine (1 Cor. 12: 3); but there are more difficult decisions than that for the community to make, and δοκιμασία, "discernment", is a vital function for them all (Rom. 12: 2; Eph. 5: 10; Phil. 1: 10; 1 Thess. 5: 21; cf. Rom. 2: 18 of Jewish moralists).[2]

All this being so, it is possible to imagine intercessions of various sorts, and likewise readings and teaching taking place in non-sacramental assemblies. It is true that the famous injunction to general petitions (including prayer for non-Christians) in 1 Tim. 2: 1 f. has been appropriated as the norm for the intercessions at Holy Communion (and is alluded to in the Prayer for the Church in the Anglican Communion Service, 1662). But there is nothing in fact to limit it to such an occasion, and it is difficult to imagine that the words "first of all", with which the injunction is introduced, are intended to relate to the position of the intercession at the beginning of the Eucharist. If this were so, what has become of the later items? "First of all" more probably means "as of foremost importance".[3]

So again there are Christian hymns in the Apocalypse; but there is nothing to prove them eucharistic—not even the "Ter Sanctus" (Rev. 4: 8; cf. Isa. 6: 2 f.) which may, as has been argued by Professor W. C. van Unnik,[4] only be an echo of the "eschatological" consciousness of all Christian worship, despite its particular association in later

[1] In *New Testament Essays* (as in Note 1, p. 3), 295.
[2] O. Cullmann, *Christ and Time*, Eng. trans., 1951, 228 f.
[3] See commentators *in loc.*
[4] "1 Clement 34 and the 'Sanctus' ", *Vigiliae Christianae*, V. 4, Oct. 1951, 204 ff.

times with the Eucharist. "Psalms and hymns and spiritual songs" (Eph. 5: 19; Col. 3: 16) must have been heard on many occasions—and incidentally, they were probably unaccompanied. Though the Temple had elaborate choirs with instrumental accompaniment, the poor and frequently clandestine Christian assemblies can hardly have boasted instruments. If stringed music (ψάλλειν) is referred to, it is "in the heart" only (Eph. 5: 19; Col. 3: 16).

Finally, as has already been observed, there is nothing to prevent our believing that homilies were delivered on many occasions and not alone at Baptism and Holy Communion. The homily in synagogue was a well-known phenomenon of Jewish worship, and both Jesus and Paul are represented as preaching in synagogues. Why should there not have been sermons and addresses also outside the synagogue and within purely Christian assemblies, even when the Sacraments were not their immediate context? And, whereas a distinctively Christian homily must, by definition, imply and spring out of the Christian Gospel, it is quite possible that, on some occasions, the preacher might assume the Gospel and concentrate on ethical teaching. There is unlikely to have been any rigid rule. What is called κήρυγμα, that is "proclamation" (of the Gospel), may be distinguished from διδαχή, the "teaching" about consequent behaviour, and these again from παράκλησις, "exhortation" to respond. *Kerygma* is obviously what, in evangelism, is directed to the outsider; but it may also occur inside the Christian assembly, by way of reminder and recapitulation; and, with or without κήρυγμα, so may διδαχή and παράκλησις. There can have been no fixed rule of "all or none".[1]

As for the arrangement and ordering of Christian assemblies, there is not much that can be said for certain, except that St. Paul evidently advocated a stern check on the activities of women in them (1 Cor. 14: 34), and that, in the Epistle of James (Jas. 2: 2–4), we get a curious picture of social distinctions and snobbery. St. Paul's strictures (1 Cor. 11: 5 ff.) on women "praying or prophesying" with bare heads still awaits a really convincing explanation. For whatever reason, he enjoined a head-covering for women in the Christian assemblies. Men, it appears from the same passage, were expected to be bareheaded; and although this is contrary to Jewish practice today (men put on a hat in synagogue), it seems that even non-Christian Jews of St. Paul's day did not necessarily cover for worship.[2]

[1] See G. Friedrich, "Fragen des Neuen Testaments an die Homiletik", *Wort und Dienst* n.F.VI, 1959, 70 ff. [2] S.-B. III, 424 f.

In the New Testament period there had not yet begun to be buildings specially designed for Christian worship, and worshippers must usually have met in private houses (cf. Acts 2: 46; 20: 9; Rom. 16: 5; Philem. 2, etc.) for distinctively Christian worship. In such circumstances there is no knowing how they disposed themselves, but there is no reason to imagine that the women were segregated, as in synagogues. The advent of church buildings no doubt made a vast difference in the organization and ordering of worship; but that is outside our period. Only in James is there any hint of distinctions of honour between various positions in the assembly place (Jas. 2: 3). In Rev. 4, it may be that the arrangements of Judaism are reflected, rather than of Christian worship.

The posture for worship was evidently sometimes kneeling (see, e.g., Luke 22: 41; Eph. 3: 14) or even prostration (Mark 14: 35; Matt. 26: 39; 1 Cor. 14: 25); but standing (often with uplifted hands) was a common attitude for prayer both in pagan and in Jewish worship (cf. Mark 11: 25; Luke 18: 11, 13), and there is no reason to doubt that Christians also adopted it from time to time (see 1 Tim. 2: 8). Looking upwards (Mark 6: 41) was an attitude for blessing God, where the modern (or at any rate Western) worshipper finds it more natural to bow the head. Perhaps bowing, kneeling, and prostration were in those days signs of special humility, intensity or anxiety.[1]

---

[1] Cf. Origen, *de orat.* (ed. E. G. Jay, 1954), xxxi.

V

THE LANGUAGE OF WORSHIP

WE HAVE SEEN evidence for various types of worship, both sacramental and non-sacramental, both more and less formal. But we have also seen that for the details of the actual words and movements all too little direct evidence is available.

On the other hand, it is difficult to avoid the impression that phrases and sometimes whole connected sections of the New Testament represent what the Christians were actually saying or singing when they were at worship. Speculation is naturally rife in so interesting and so uncertain a field, and it would be wrong to dogmatize. It has already been said, for instance (p. 58 above), that the evidence for an actual liturgy underlying 1 Peter is less secure than it is sometimes held to be. But it may be of value to mention here briefly some of the other New Testament passages claimed, sometimes with more, sometimes with less cogency, to contain liturgical echoes.[1]

And first, allusion should be made to the theory, worked out in detail by the late A. C. MacPherson,[2] that St. John's Gospel contains traditions of how John ("the elder"?) prayed and preached when celebrating the Eucharist. The presumption is that a leading member of the Ephesian Church, possessed of very vivid traditions about the words and deeds of Jesus—if not actually himself an acquaintance of the Lord—might weave into his extempore eucharistic "*propheteia*"—his prayer and discourse—an extended meditation on the mission and work of Christ, in a form in which he as it were (though with complete reverence) impersonated Christ. Christ was the unseen Celebrant, and the disciple or elder, uttering the eucharistic prayers and praises and discourse, drew upon the very words which had come down in the living traditions as Christ's own words on the eve of His betrayal. The whole Gospel may have grown up round such worship. There is some possibility that the story of Christ's death was often recited at the Eucharist (cf. perhaps 1 Cor. 11: 26); it might be that this extended

[1] There is a bibliography in Delling, as in Note 1, p. 8 .
[2] A posthumous edition of his work is imminent.

meditation is the deposit of the kind of things that were said on such occasions.

St. Matthew's Gospel may well, it has been claimed, represent a collection of the kind of teachings and anecdotes that were read or told at assemblies for worship;[1] and Archbishop P. Carrington has argued that Mark is related to the Jewish lectionary tradition and to the primitive Christian calendar.[2] Strength is lent to this type of theory by Justin's allusion to apostolic ἀπομνημονεύματα, reminiscences, used at worship.[3] But one is bound to observe that the Gospels seem really far more suitable for apologetic purposes;[4] and the same applies also to the Acts. More recently Professor A. Guilding has put forward her theory that St. John's Gospel is a kind of Christian commentary on the Jewish lections (see Note 1, p. 14). The Epistles, it has already been noted (p. 43 above) might possibly have provided, at least in some instances, a kind of apostolic homily to precede the Eucharist.

The Apocalypse, some have held, is built round forms of Jewish worship developed in a Christian manner. Certainly it contains many psalm-like Christian hymns (Christian "enthronement Psalms" acclaiming God and Christ as King).[5]

This raises the question of the influence of the Jewish lectionary and the Jewish festal calendar on Christian worship, a matter of very considerable moment which still awaits a detailed answer. The evolution of the Christian calendar and its relation to the Jewish calendar is discussed by A. A. MacArthur (as in Note 1, p. 17). On the Jewish lectionary, valuable work was done by A. Büchler and, following in his footsteps, H. St. J. Thackeray. Contemporary writers are returning to the investigation.[6] But the variations of the lectionary in different groups and over different areas in New Testament times remain matter for speculation and further research; and the degrees of its influence on Christian worship are still to be explored. It is clear enough that Ps. 34,

---

[1] See G. D. Kilpatrick, *The Origins of the Gospel according to St. Matthew*, 1946.

[2] P. Carrington, *The Primitive Christian Calendar*, 1952. The difficulties in accepting this theory are exposed by W. D. Davies in *The Background*, etc. (as in Note 1, p. 3'1), 124 ff.

[3] *Apol.* i. 67.

[4] C. F. D. Moule in *New Testament Essays* (as in Note 1, p. 3), 165 ff.

[5] See, e.g., discussions of their rhythm, etc., by E. Lohmeyer in his commentary (*Lietzmann, Handbuch zum N.T.*, revised ed. 1953).

[6] A. Büchler, *Jewish Quarterly Review* V. 1893, 420 ff., VI. 1894, 1 ff.; H. St. J. Thackeray, *The Septuagint and Jewish Worship* (Schweich Lectures, 1920).

for instance, lies behind 1 Peter: but the implications of this for the occasion of the epistle are far from clear.[1]

Incidentally, it is a debatable point (as has been already said) whether the Jews of Christ's day used the whole Psalter, or whether they were not far more judiciously selective than the Anglican Church has been. That Christian worship was strongly influenced by certain Psalms, however, is clear enough; and that worshippers were often capable of extemporizing in a Psalm-like manner is likely. Whatever the origin of the Lukan canticles (whether they are of pre-Christian Baptist origin or are a reminiscence of what was actually said at the time or a Lukan composition),[2] this kind of composition may well have occurred at Christian worship from time to time. "Psalms and hymns and spiritual songs" perhaps merged into one another, without always very clear boundaries to mark the end of quotation and the beginning of free composition. One longs to know what it was that Pliny referred to (*Epp.* x. 96) as "singing a hymn to Christ as God". It is quite possible that pagan hymnic style, as well as Jewish psalmody, influenced the Christian hymns.[3]

Among the claimants to recognition as distinctively Christian hymnody in the New Testament—to come now to possible fragments of liturgy—are obviously Eph. 5: 14 and 1 Tim. 3: 16. But similar claims have also been made for Col. 1: 15–20, for the meditation on Christ's humility in Phil. 2; for 2 Tim. 2: 11–13; and for 1 Pet. 3: 18–22.[4] In Acts 4: 24–31 there is a sudden outburst of praise, psalmody, and

---

[1] For investigations of this kind, see J. van Goudoever, as in Note 1, p. 12, and A. Guilding, as in Note 1, p. 9 .

[2] See suggestions by P. Winter, "Magnificat and Benedictus—Maccabaean Psalms?", *B.J.R.L.* 37. 1, 1954, 328 ff.

[3] See a discussion of this in Delling, as in Note 1, p. 8, and note the description of the Therapeutae in Philo *vit. cont.* 80, there cited.

[4] Col. 1: 15–20: e.g. C. Masson, 1950, *in loc.*, and in *Revue de Théologie et de Philosophie*, CXLVIII, 1948, and J. M. Robinson, "A Formal Analysis of Colossians 1: 15–20", *J.B.L.* LXXVI. 4, 1957, 270 ff. Also (1: 13–20) E. Käsemann, "Eine urchristliche Taufliturgie (Kol. 1: 13–20)", *Festschr. für R. Bultmann*, 1949, 133 ff. Phil. 2: 6–11: e.g. E. Lohmeyer, *Kyrios Jesus*, in *Sitz.d.Heidelb.Akad.d. Wiss., Phil.-Hist.Klasse*, IV, 1927–8, and F. W. Beare, 1959, *in loc.* 2 Tim. 2: 11–13: commentaries *in loc.* 1 Pet. 3: 18–22: e.g. R. Bultmann (as in Note 3, p. 17), 505, and J. Coutts, "Ephesians 1, 3–14 and 1 Peter 1, 3–12", *J.N.T.S.* III. 2, 1957, 115 ff.

Add Eph. 1: 3–14: e.g. T. Innitzer, "Der Hymnus im Epheserbriefe 1, 3–14", *Zeitsch. für Kathol.Theol.*, 1904, 612 ff.; H. Coppieters, "La Doxologie de la Lettre aux Éphésiens," *R.B.*, 1909, 74 ff.; E. Lohmeyer, "Das Proömium des

petition, which is suggestive of the way in which all kinds of elements —borrowed and original—may have become fused together in the spontaneity of early Christian worship. For this very reason it is impossible to establish with any certainty that this or that is an actual "hymn" in the sense of a fixed composition often repeated in the same form. Most of the attempts to discover regularity and strophic symmetry are rather arbitrary. The fact is that, in the very nature of the case, Christian writing of the sort we know in the New Testament welled up from a great fund of poetry and prose which was all of a piece with the common worship of the Christian communities: and it as as hopeless to "categorize" in such conditions as it is to represent a galloping horse by one "still" from a motion picture. Paul and Silas actually prayed and "hymned" God while they were in the stocks in the Philippian gaol (Acts 16: 25): the whole thing must have been spontaneous and natural in the extreme.

What were the characteristic forms of words and phrases used in Christian praise and prayer? One generalization can be made, namely that in the New Testament the usual manner is to praise God for Jesus Christ or to pray to Him through Jesus Christ rather than to address Christ directly. Direct address to the risen Christ in prayer or praise is seldom to be found in the New Testament. Stephen at the hour of his martyrdom (Acts 7: 59) cries "Lord Jesus, receive my spirit!"—a very striking phrase, especially when it is compared and contrasted with "Father, into thy hands I commend my spirit." Similarly Paul on the Damascus Road (Acts 22: 10) says "What shall I do, Lord?"; and in Acts 22: 19 he is represented as describing a dialogue with Christ in a subsequent vision, in which he again addresses him as "Lord". Possibly the allusion in 2 Cor. 12: 8 to his beseeching "the Lord" for the removal of the "thorn in the flesh" is also intended to indicate address to Christ, though this is not certain. Most cogent of all, however, is the Aramaic phrase *Marana tha* (1 Cor. 16: 22; *Didache* 10: 6) which—if the words are rightly thus divided—bears witness to a very ancient invocation of Christ. *Marana tha* means "O, our Lord, come!" and would thus correspond to the Greek phrase in Rev. 22: 20, "Amen, come Lord Jesus!" It is true that Bultmann has argued[1] that *Marana* may originally have been intended to designate God, but it is most unlikely that this held for Christian usage. It is true also that the

Epheserbriefes," *Theol. Blätter*, 1926, coll. 120 ff.; N. A. Dahl, "Adresse und Proömium des Epheserbriefes", *Theol. Zeitschr.*, 1951, 241 ff.; J. Coutts, as above.

[1] As in Note 3, p. 17; 54 f.

Aramaic words may be divided otherwise—*Maran atha*—so as to make the phrase a statement, "Our Lord has come", instead of a prayer (cf. Phil. 4: 5, "the Lord is at hand"). But since the Greek phrase in Rev. 22: 20 is unambiguously in the imperative, not the indicative, a good case can be made for *Marana tha*[1] as the earliest known invocation to Christ. Whether it is eucharistic is another matter.[2] Finally, the phrase "those who invoke the Name (of Christ)" as a description of Christians ought also perhaps to be included in the evidence (see Acts 2: 21; 9: 14, 21; 22: 16; Rom. 10: 12 f.; 1 Cor. 1: 2).

Much commoner, however, is prayer, praise, or adoration addressed to God *through* or *in the name of* Christ.[3] Prayer to God in the name of Christ implies that worshippers may now approach into the very presence of the Almighty with new confidence ($\pi\alpha\rho\rho\eta\sigma\iota\alpha$) because the death of Christ has torn the separating curtain which hitherto had excluded from direct approach. In this sense, Christ's own "flesh" is a new way into the presence of God—a way which is "alive", for the way *is* the living Christ: incorporate in His humanity our humanity now enters the presence of God (Heb. 10: 20). Or again, it implies that, although personally unworthy, we are able to return into the family of God because of the costly forgiveness offered by God Himself and put into effect in the death of Christ: God in Christ has reconciled us; therefore it is through Christ that we draw near. Or yet again, it is the same Spirit of God who in Jesus of Nazareth cried "Abba! Father!" (the cry of absolute obedience) who now cries "Abba! Father!" in us; so that it is "through Christ" that the Holy Spirit works in our wills enabling us to draw near to God (Mark 14: 36; Rom. 8: 15; Gal. 4: 6).

All this, and more besides, is implied by the formula "through Jesus Christ", which presumably figured in early Christian prayers as it demonstrably did in early Christian greetings and expressions of good wishes,[4] and which is evidently in view in John 16: 23–27. There Jesus is represented as saying that the disciples are to make requests of the Father "in his name". In *vv.* 26 f. it is emphasized that they need not use Jesus as an intermediary, for the Father Himself loves them and they may make requests direct to God. But the requests are still to be "in

---

[1] Though S.-B. III 494 argue against the division *marana tha*.

[2] See Note 3, p. 39.

[3] Those who constantly use the verbless phrase "In the name of the Father and of the Son and of the Holy Ghost, Amen" are invited at this point to ask themselves what they mean by it.

[4] W. Heitmüller, as in Note 2, p. 48, etc.

the name of" Jesus—that is, by virtue of this bridge which God has Himself thrown across to man in Jesus Christ. Apparently it is prayer "in the name of" Christ which is also alluded to in 2 Cor. 1: 19 f. There St. Paul is arguing that a true Christian cannot be fickle and irresponsible in his planning, as though, in his own right, he might say first "Yes" and then "No", because his concern is not man's choices but God's plan; and Christ Himself is a steady and consistent "Yes" to all God's promises: "that, too", St. Paul continues, "is why the 'Amen' is uttered by us through Christ, to God's glory". The whole passage contains subtle allusions to the Hebrew root 'MN (from which "Amen" is derived), which stands for consistency, affirmation, positiveness; and it looks as though at its climax St. Paul is appealing to recognized liturgical practice. He is saying, in effect, "You know that we say 'through Jesus Christ our Lord. Amen': well, the reason is that that affirmation 'Amen', is all summed up in Christ and guaranteed by Him". (For Christ as Himself "the Amen", cf. Rev. 3: 14.)[1]

Evidently, then, prayers "through Jesus Christ" were current in the worship of New Testament times. A variant of this usage—differing scarcely at all in sense—is actually to be found in Eph. 3: 14-21, where the noble prayer is crowned with a doxology, that is, an ascription of glory to God, "in the church and in Christ Jesus" (so the best text). This means, apparently, that the medium through which glory may be offered to God is the worshipping Christian community, which, in its turn, is so closely identified with Christ, as His Body, that, in the same breath, the medium may be described as Christ Jesus Himself.

In view of this it is the more amazing that the doxology of the Lord's prayer is totally devoid of the Christian formula.[2]

The name of Jesus was not only used in petition or in ascription; it occurred also, no doubt, in allusions in the course of primitive Christian benedictions. Just as in Jewish liturgy God was adored and praised with reference to His mighty deeds in creation and in the triumph of the Exodus, so for the Christian worshipper the new Exodus, the new "Paschal event" in Christ, was at the centre of every act of praise. A very free and rambling form of such an act of praise, merging into petition, is to be found in Acts 4: 24b-30, already alluded to, a passage which illustrates a remarkable number of the component parts of the language of Christian worship. The address to God as δεσπότης is a

---

[1] See W. C. van Unnik, "Reisepläne und Amensagen . . ." in *Studia Paulina* (as in Note 1, p. 52), 215 ff.
[2] See C. F. D. Moule (as in Note 1, p. 37), 253 f.

reverential opening, rare in the New Testament (elsewhere only Luke 2: 29; Rev. 6: 10; cf. 2 Pet. 2: 1, unless this last is intended to refer to Christ, but frequent in 1 Clem., and occurring also in Barnabas, Diognetus and Hermas; and there are plenty of examples in the LXX, for *Adon*, etc.). Then follows a characteristically Jewish allusion to the creation, and then a Christian application of Psalm 2, which introduces a reference to God's "servant" (παῖς) David, which is forthwith paralleled by reference to His "holy servant" (ἅγιος παῖς) Jesus (vv. 27, 30). This parallelism makes it highly probable that the term παῖς, "servant", is here intended to be a royal term (a Davidic title) rather than an allusion to the suffering servant of Isa. 53 (though it may be that the suffering servant is intended in Acts 3: 13, in a different context). If so, we have an interesting parallel to this use of παῖς Δαυείδ side by side with παῖς Ἰησοῦς in Didache 9: 2, suggesting that early Christian prayer fell, at times, into a pattern already formed by Jewish liturgical practice. It is the Eucharistic benediction (exemplified perhaps by Didache 9 just quoted) which provides the most obvious and most important "allusive" use of the name of Jesus. That it should be called "benediction" rather than "thanksgiving" is the point made by J.-P. Audet in his commentary on the Didache and mentioned earlier in this discussion (p. 42 above).

Thus, address direct to Christ is rare in the New Testament; but address to God *through* Christ and benediction of God *for* His mighty deeds in Christ were normal.

The "Amen" has already been alluded to.[1] It is a Semitic word, connected with a root meaning firmness, consistency, truthfulness, and already in the Old Testament it appears frequently enough as a formula of confirmation, whether in the acceptance of an oath (Num. 5: 22, etc.), or in the affirmation of praise to God—the God who is Himself "the God of Amen" (Isa. 65: 16). Thus it often comes at the end of doxologies (Ps. 41: 13; 89: 52 (twice); 106: 48 (with a liturgical "stage direction"), etc., etc.); and in synagogue worship, if not before (cf. Neh. 8: 6), it became the people's response to the leader's expressions of worship—for instance, at the end of each clause of the "Aaronic blessing", Num. 6: 24–26. It was, that is to say, the congregation's audible appropriation of what was said on their behalf—a deeper, much more devotional, God-centred counterpart to a secular "Hear! hear!" Occasionally also it was used to emphasize and, as it were, to clinch one's own prayer. In Tobit 8: 5–7, Tobit utters a prayer, and at the

[1] For what follows, see H. Schlier *s.v.* in *T.W.N.T.*

end of it (*v.* 8) Sarah says "Amen" *with* him. Thus it is that (as all the Gospel traditions attest), Jesus Himself used the word to emphasize particularly weighty and solemn sayings of His own, placing it at the *beginning*, not at the end, and (if the Johannine tradition is correct) doubling it: "Amen, amen I say . . ." (cf. Neh. 8: 6 again). This initial Amen, very striking as it must have been, may well have added impetus to the Church's use, although the Church has not generally placed it at the beginning of a phrase.

At any rate, Amen is well attested in the New Testament and the Apostolic Fathers. With doxologies it occurs at Rom. 1: 25; 9: 5; 11: 36; 16: 27; Gal. 1: 5; Eph. 3: 21; Phil. 4: 20; 1 Tim. 1: 17; 6: 16; 2 Tim. 4; 18; Heb. 13: 21; 1 Pet. 4: 11; 5: 11; Jude 25; and in the majestic description of worship in heaven in Rev. 5, the four living creatures utter "Amen" to the praise uplifted by the myriads of angels. Again, in Rev. 7: 12 it both closes one ascription of praise (*v.* 10) and opens another; and at the very end (22: 20), to the solemn assurance "Yes (ναί), I am coming soon" the reply is "Amen, come, Lord Jesus!"

Amen is thus one of the most ubiquitous of the transliterations from a Semitic language which have embedded themselves in worship. Already in the LXX it occasionally appears transliterated, though more often it is translated by γένοιτο or sometimes ἀληθῶς, while in Aquila's version it appears generally as πεπιστωμένως. In the New Testament, most often transliterated, it is sometimes translated. Luke sometimes renders it by ἀληθῶς (9: 27; 12: 44; 21: 3) or ἐπ᾽ ἀληθείας (4: 25); and in Rev. 1: 7 (ναί, amen) Greek and Semitic stand side by side, while in Rev. 22: 20 just cited "Yes (ναί), I am coming soon", is answered by "Amen, come, Lord Jesus!" In the passage discussed earlier, 2 Cor. 1: 15 ff., several Greek words are used with allusion to the "Amen" which is, as it were, the "text" of the meditation: "Yes" (ναί), "faithful" (πιστός), "confirming" (βεβαιῶν).[1]

But if there is ample material in the New Testament to illustrate the force of Amen, the only specific allusions to its use actually in Christian worship are in two passages. The passage just cited culminates (2 Cor. 1: 20) in the words: "therefore also the Amen is uttered to God's glory by us through Christ". And in 1 Cor. 14: 16 St. Paul asks how the uninstructed person (ἰδιώτης) can be expected to say "the Amen" to a thanksgiving uttered in a "tongue", that is, it would seem, an inarticulate, ecstatic ejaculation intelligible only to such as were spiritually *en*

[1] See Note I, p. 67.

rapport with the speaker. However, it was probably common, and Justin (*Apol.* i. 65) mentions the Amen to the celebrant's eucharistic prayer as a regular feature: "when he has finished the prayers and the thanksgiving, the whole people there assents, ἐπευφημεῖ 'Amen'. In Hebrew 'Amen' means 'so be it!'"

In the main, then, the liturgical use of Amen is as the congregation's appropriation and confirmation of what has been uttered on their behalf by the leader of the worship. There is less logic in the use of it at the end of what has been said or sung by the whole company (as Amen is often sung at the end of a hymn today—cf., again, Rev. 7: 12—and as it is used sometimes in Jewish liturgy also), although this too (as has been seen) can be justified as a reaffirmation, redundant but, sparingly used, effective.[1]

Foreign words in liturgy constitute an interesting study. Besides "Amen", some, at least, of the Greek-speaking communities of the New Testament period used *Marana tha*, as we have seen, apparently as an invocation, possibly at the Eucharist (but see Note 3, p. 44 above). In 1 Cor. 16: 22 *Maranatha* is closely accompanied by the word *Anathema* (for a suggested reason, see same Note). *Anathema*, unlike its companion, is a Greek word. It means "an accursed object", something or someone placed under the ban (in the LXX it represents *herem*). Its other occurrences in the New Testament are in Rom. 9: 3; Gal. 1: 8 f. and Acts 23: 14. In 1 Cor. 16: 22 its object is "anyone who does not love the Lord"; in Gal. 1: 8 f. it is anyone who brings a false Gospel; and in Rom. 9: 3 St. Paul declares that he himself is ready to fall under the ban of exclusion from Christ, if only that could save his fellow Jews. The Acts example is not relevant for our purposes. The *anathema* was thus evidently a formula of excommunication (in the case of one already within the community) or of exclusion (in the case of one attempting to enter illegitimately). If 1 Cor. 16: 22 is intended (like *Didache* 10: 6, according to J.-P. Audet, etc.) to mark the beginning of the Eucharist proper, then we may have here early examples of "the fencing of the table"—the solemn exclusion of all except Christians in full communion. To judge by Rev. 19 Christians also used (as we still do) the cry "(h)allelu-Jah", "praise ye Jah!". "*Hosanna*" (a rough transliteration of the Hebrew for "Save, we pray!" from Ps. 118: 25) may also have been current. In the New Testament it occurs only in the accounts of the Triumphal entry in Matt. (21: 9, 15), Mark (11: 9 f.),

[1] Note the final Amen to books of the N.T. in the *textus receptus*; and see the Jewish *Authorized Daily Prayer Book* (tr. S. Singer, ed. I. Abrahams, 1914), e.g. p. 14.

and John (12: 13); but in the *Didache* (10: 6) it appears in liturgical use and it may have been so used at an early date, perhaps as a shout of acclamation rather than as a conscious prayer for divine help.

One other Semitic word has a particularly interesting history, namely *Abba*. In the Gospels it occurs only once, in the Markan account of Christ's "agony" (that is, struggle or contest) in the Garden of Gethsemane. There (14: 36), at the very climax of this titanic battle of obedience against all the powers of disobedience, Jesus cries "Abba, Father, everything is possible for thee: let this cup pass from me. Yet not my will but thine be done." Now it seems to be established that, whereas "Abba" was a common enough form among the contemporaries of Jesus when a child addressed his father, it is unexampled as the address of a worshipper to his heavenly Father. In such cases the same root ('B) would be used, but a different, more formal termination (*abinu*, "our Father", and so forth). If so, Jesus is here portrayed as using, in prayer to God, an address of the most daring intimacy—and that, not in order to take the liberties of familiarity but, on the contrary, to express the most costly form of absolute submission: "not my will but thine be done". Just as Christ seems seldom to have spoken of God as King or Lord but often as Father, so here His address to God is on the very simplest level of family relationships, and, at one and the same time, on the profoundest level of reverence and obedience: thus a new epoch is marked in the history of prayer to God.

It is therefore the more remarkable that St. Paul can claim that exactly the same approach to God is made possible for Christians by the Holy Spirit: Rom. 8: 15; Gal. 4: 6. These two Pauline passages suggest that the actual Aramaic word used by Jesus Himself was retained in the prayer language of the early Greek-speaking Churches, even though side by side with the Greek equivalent;[1] and that whenever the Lord's Prayer, perhaps, as will be noted below, beginning "Abba! Father!", was uttered with sincerity this was one of the signs of the real presence of the Holy Spirit in the Church. Indeed, the absolute obedience it implied could be achieved only in the power of that same Spirit who was at work in Jesus.

One other liturgical phrase must be mentioned here, namely "for ever and ever", εἰς τοὺς αἰῶνας τῶν αἰώνων (and variants).[2] This,

---

[1] *Contra* S. V. McCasland, " 'Abba, Father' ", *J.B.L.* LXXII, 1953, 79 ff.

[2] See *T.W.N.T.* I. 198 f.; note Matt. 6: 13; John 4: 14; Eph. 3: 21 (cf. Col. 1: 26); Heb. 1: 8; 5: 6; 2 Pet. 3: 18; Jude 13, 25; also *Joseph and Aseneth*, editions as in Note 4, p. 17, and Note 3, p. 18.

although constituted by Greek words, is clearly derived from Semitic phrases such as *le 'olam wa'ed*, and must be reckoned among the legacies of Judaism. The English rendering "world without end" is correspondingly odd. No doubt the Semitic words spring from the essentially Hebraic tendency to think of the ideal world under the images of time even more than of space. Instead of a Platonic "other world", the Hebrews thought rather in terms of a "further age".

To return to the Lord's Prayer, a good case can be made for the view that the prayer taught by Jesus to His friends opened with that very word *Abba*, that intimate, child-like form of address. One is often told that Jesus taught His disciples to use a different form of address to God from the one He Himself used; as though He emphasized the "ye" in "when ye pray, say 'Our Father in heaven' . . ." But a comparative and critical study of the best texts of the Lord's Prayer in Matthew and Luke makes it probable that the earliest Greek form was simply πάτερ; and the evidence of Rom. 8 and Gal. 4 for the currency of a similar phrase is confirmatory.[1] One may add that there is no need to find, as is sometimes found, allusion to a difference between Jesus and His disciples in this respect in the phrase, John 20: 17, "Your Father and my Father, your God and my God"; for this need only mean "Your Father *who is also mine*. . . ." It seems that a reconstruction of the Lord's Prayer attained by critical inspection of the synoptic tradition would be something like the following: "Father, hallowed be thy name; thy kingdom come; give us today the bread that we need (or the bread of the morrow); and forgive us our debts, as we also have forgiven our debtors; and lead us not into temptation."[2] But if the doxology is a later addition, it is very remarkable (as has been said) that it contains no distinctively Christian formula. Can the explanation be that, after all, Jesus Himself did use some sort of doxology, and that, out of reverence for His words, the Christian Church never substantially altered it?[3]

If what has been said about *Abba* is true, it is a curious fact that this, the most intimate of all prayer-words, should by its very transplantation into the setting of an alien language, Greek, have been on the way to becoming a crystallized "liturgical formula". Not that there is direct

---

[1] T. W. Manson, "The Lord's Prayer", *B.J.R.L.* 38.1 (Sept. 1955), 104 f.; A. R. George, as in Note 1, p. 10; J. Jeremias, "The Lord's Prayer in Modern Research", *E.T.* LXXI. 5, Feb. 1960, 141 ff. *Contra*, G. Bornkamm, *Jesus of Nazareth* (Eng. trans. 1960), 128 f.

[2] See previous note.   [3] See C. F. D. Moule (as in Note 1, p. 37), 253 f.

evidence for this. But one cannot help imagining that it soon began to sound as archaic and mysterious as, let us say, *Kyrie eleison* does in English liturgy.

The question of the right liturgical language is an important and difficult one. It is likely that even the most spontaneous early Christian prayer was in part stylized and formalized by Old Testament and Jewish formulae, just as extempore prayer today is often strongly flavoured by the Authorized Version. Ancient and modern, prose and poetry, the elevated and the ordinary, very probably went hand in hand. And although such combinations are in a way uneasy and un-pleasant to the ear, it is doubtful whether either side can be dispensed with in Christian worship. The ideal is perhaps when a number of small "cells" or groups of Christians are learning to pray together with complete informality and in their own words, while they also come together weekly for the more formal, more dignified public worship of the whole Christian assembly for the area.

While there are very few prayers in completely contemporary and natural English which sound sufficiently dignified for public corporate worship, yet, if such prayer were not in constant use side by side with the other, the loss in spontaneity and intimacy and reality might be very serious indeed. Conversely, although one may well ask what place such alien words as *Abba, Amen, Maranatha, Hallelujah, Agnus Dei, Kyrie eleison, Benedictus* have in the reformed worship of rational people, one is bound to ask, on the other hand, whether it is possible to eliminate from worship the mysterious, the elevated, the unusual, without corresponding loss. Incidentally, it is worth noting that not only did Greek forms of Christian worship borrow Semitic words, but Jewish worship (possibly before Christ) conversely borrowed Greek.[1]

With regard to doxologies, blessings, ascriptions, greetings and the like in the New Testament, one observation too seldom made is that the current habit of almost always using an optative or imperative in translations of such phrases seems to be contrary to the balance of New Testament usage. The present tendency is to say "Glory be to God!" "The Lord be with you!" Hebrew and Biblical Greek more often than not omit the verb altogether; but where a verb is supplied, it is as often as not in the indicative. Admittedly, in what might be assumed[2] to be

---

[1] M.-J. Lagrange, *Épître aux Galates*, 1918, 105, cites *mari kiri* (see Mark 14: 36 with L's comment there), "comme qui dirait: 'mon seigneur, signor mio' ", and *kiri mari abi* (*Shemoth. rabb.* 140, 2).

[2] Wrongly? See W. C. van Unnik, as in Note 1, p. 3.

the prototype of the "salutation"—Ruth 2: 4—Boaz, using a verbless phrase, "Yahweh with you!" is replied to with, "May Yahweh bless thee!" (a mood of wishing). Admittedly, also, the regular Hebrew opening to a benediction (*baruch*=Greek εὐλογητός) is a verbless participle which may be a wish or a statement. But to set against this there are such unequivocal indicatives as "Grace, mercy, and peace shall be with us" (2 John 3), "Thine is the kingdom . . ." (Matt. 6: 13 *v. l.*); and a list of New Testament formulae of this sort reveals that the verb is most often unexpressed, but, when expressed, is not seldom in the indicative.[1] This suggests that some element of confident affirmation has been lost from worship since New Testament times.

Finally, there is something to be learnt from the words used in the Bible for worship. As a condition of worship there must be awe—a sense of the "numinous", of the mysterious—a feeling sometimes indicated in the New Testament by θάμβος, when the more than human majesty of Jesus is felt and recognized (cf. the Old Testament *pachad*, etc.). Crudely and physically determined, one of its symptoms may be "gooseflesh": the demons "shudder" (φρίσσειν) at the recognition of the God whom they fear (Jas. 2: 19). But when this passes beyond the immediate sense of terror to an adoring reverence, there naturally follow gestures, movements, and attitudes of reverence.

The word προσκυνεῖν, and its chief Hebrew counterpart, *hishtachawoth.*, strictly apply, it seems, to outward gestures of worship— προσκυνεῖν sometimes meaning "to kiss" (probably its original mean-

---

[1] Cf. van Unnik, as last Note, 283. The distribution is (with slight variations dependent upon text) as follows:

No main verb: Lk. 1: 68; Rom. 1: 7, 9: 5, 15: 33, 16: 27; 1 Cor. 1: 3, 16: 23 f.; 2 Cor. 1: 2, 13: 14; Gal. 1: 3, 5, 6: 16, 18; Eph. 1: 2 f., 3: 20 f., 6: 23 f.; Phil. 1: 2, 4: 23; Col. 1: 2, 4: 18; 1 Thess. 1: 1, 5: 28; 2 Thess. 1: 2, 3: 18; 1 Tim. 1: 2, 17, 6: 16, 21; 2 Tim. 1: 2, 4: 18, 22; Tit. 1: 4, 3: 15; Philem. 3, 25; Heb. 13: 21b, 25; 1 Pet. 1: 3, 5: 14; 2 Pet. 3: 18; 3 John 14; Jude 24 f.; Rev. 1: 4, 6, 5: 13, 7: 12, 15: 3 (see also indic.) 19: 1 (see also indic.), 22: 21 (total about 50).

Optative or Imperative: Matt. 6: 9, 10; Rom. 15: 13; 1 Thess. 3: 11 f. 5: 23; 2 Thess. 2: 16 f., 3: 5; Heb. 13: 20, 21a; 1 Pet. 1: 2; 2 Pet. 1: 2; Jude 2; Rev. 19: 7 (virtually) (total about 11).

Indicative: Matt. 6: 13 (*v. l.*); 2 Cor. 11: 31 (ὁ ὤν); Phil. 4: 7, 9; 1 Pet. 4: 11, 5: 10; 2 John 3; Rev. 4: 11, 5: 9, 12, 11: 15, 17 f., 12: 10 f. (virtually), 15: 3, 19: 1 (virtually: see also no verb), 6 ff. (total about 16).

The fact that *amen* (at least in some readings) closes a good many of these phrases may be supposed to turn in an optative direction some which are verbless; but I doubt if this follows. See the remarks on *amen*, pp. 73–75.

ing), and then "to bow" or "prostrate oneself", which is also what the Hebrew word means. These words are used of obeisance before men as well as before God. But they come to denote, more generally, "worship", as in John 4: 20–23—the only New Testament passage where the noun προσκυνηταί, "worshippers", appears.

In addition to this word-group, there are words denoting the use of the voice in worship. Vocal worship involves something very near to "benediction" in the sense in which it has been defined earlier. If so, Luke 24: 53 (εὐλογεῖν) and Acts 2: 47 (αἰνεῖν) are the most obvious New Testament passages referring to this occupation—and that, in the Temple. But privately also, among themselves, the Christians "lifted up their voice to God" (Acts 4: 24); and elsewhere we read of "hymning" and "singing" (Acts 16: 25; Eph. 5: 19, etc.).

But much of what is generally meant by worship in ordinary Christian usage—and certainly in the title of this book—over and above the express utterance of benedictions, is represented in the New Testament vocabulary by λειτουργία and λατρεία, "service". The modern Christian application of terms such as "divine service" or "a service" to specific acts of public worship may tend to obscure the fact that in its New Testament context the word "service" does literally mean the work of servants. One of the regular Hebrew words for worship, 'abodah, is derived from the same root as the word for the suffering "servant" or, for that matter, any slave or servant. It is used in Exodus for the hard servitude of the Hebrews under Pharaoh. Another Hebrew word, sharath, which is used of "ministering" in the Temple (particularly with reference to the specialized ministry of priests and Levites) is also used of domestic service (on a higher level than the menial). And in the New Testament the two groups of words, λατρεία, λατρεύειν (in Rom. 9: 4 ἡ λατρεία, "the service", is used absolutely, to mean the whole system of Jewish worship in the Temple), and λειτουργία, λειτουργός, λειτουργεῖν, both concern simply the rendering of service—the latter, in secular literature, having behind it a long history of service to the state, and being used in the New Testament of service to men as well as to God.

Thus there is inherent in the Biblical conception of worship something active and strenuous; and although the Christian gospel of God's initiative and of His wholly unmerited and unearned graciousness has quite transformed the meaning of any "offering" of "service" which can be rendered by men to God, yet the terms still present a salutary bulwark against slovenly or supine conceptions. God is described, in a famous prayer, as the God whose *service* (i.e. slavery) is perfect freedom (cf. Rom. 6: 18).

On the other hand, the New Testament does not use in this connexion the words θεραπεύειν, θεράπων, of which the noun is common in the Greek Old Testament, and both noun and verb in pagan writings for the service of the gods. In the New Testament, in Acts 17: 25 St. Paul is represented as repudiating the idea that the sublime Creator requires such service (θεραπεύειν) from human hands; in Hebrews 3: 5 Moses is called a θεράπων in God's household. Otherwise this root is used in the NewTestament only of *"therapy"*— of "healing" the sick; and only rarely is it used in the Greek Old Testament for the service of God. Is it possible that the reason for this avoidance may be precisely that these words might by this time have conveyed the impression that man can confer a benefit on God by his service? Christian worship is indeed service—hard work—but it is the responsive service of obedience and of gratitude, not of flattery or of "mutual benefit".

EPILOGUE

THE LAST CHAPTER ended with the observation that, although the God and Father of our Lord Jesus Christ cannot be bribed by offerings and does not depend upon our services, yet there is no better way in which the gratitude of the redeemed can be expressed than in costly, hard-working "service", so that words connoting the labour of servants and the expenditure of whatever is precious are rightly appropriated for worship.[1]

Worship is work. But, conversely, all work done and all life lived for God's sake is, in essence, worship. That there is any distinction at all between worship and work, or, for that matter, any other aspect of life, is due only to the fact that we are creatures of successiveness, moving in time and space, and unable to concentrate on more than a little at a time. In heaven there can be no such distinction:

> There dawns no Sabbath, no Sabbath is o'er,
> Those Sabbath-keepers have one and no more;
> One and unending is that triumph-song
> Which to the Angels and us shall belong.[2]

But here on earth it is necessary to set aside specific times for the rendering to God of articulate praise and for the conscious dedication to Him of our whole life and work. Although ideally there is truth in Origen's remark,[3] "for the perfect Christian each day is a Lord's day", yet, as someone else has wisely said, the surest way to profane the whole week would be to try to make every day equally holy. Since we live

---

[1] Perhaps this is the right place to protest against the stupid phrase "let us make an act of . . ." which has become common in the "biddings" of special services. The Latin idiom *agere gratias, paenitentiam*, "to render thanks", "to show penitence", may, conceivably, be rightly though unidiomatically translated "to make an act of thanksgiving, of penitence", if the intention is to stress the active, strenuous nature of the undertaking; but to extend the unEnglish phrase to other objects which in Latin are not used with *agere*, seems to be gratuitous, to say the least.

[2] Abelard, tr. J. M. Neale (English Hymnal no. 465).

[3] *Contra Celsum* viii. 22.

within the narrow limits of human capacities, the only practical way to hallow the whole is to bring a token portion of it consciously to God. As with the Jewish ritual of the offering of the firstfruits to hallow the entire crop, or of the sabbath to hallow the whole week, so it is with the Christian Sunday and with specific places and actions in worship. In these is concentrated the offering of all our time and space—all our being and possessions—in praise to God. Moreover, it is obviously vital for the Church, represented by the Christian congregation in a given area, to assemble *together* for worship; and that can only take place if there are specific times and agreed places for assembly. The New Testament seems to set considerable store by coming *together* (ἐπὶ τὸ αὐτό) all in one place.

This principle is integral with revealed religion generally. It is in keeping with that specialization—at first sight so puzzling, but on reflection so obviously essential—which is found in the election of Israel, or, more particularly, in the incarnation itself (the greatest "scandal of particularity"), and in the whole sacramental principle. God, as it were, focuses His entire being at particular points of intense light and heat, that we may see, and feel, and appropriate.

There lies the only justification for describing as "divine service" in particular those representative "liturgical" acts which, in fact, are the token that all life is strenuously offered to God as "divine service" and as "liturgy"; and it is death to Christian worship when, forgetting this, we allow it to become detached from life. There is a deep truth in E. Schweizer's summing up: "In the New Testament community there is no longer any 'cultus' in the ancient sense."[1] To revert to a specialized cultus means incurring the peril of over-formalization, which may sever that essential contact, just as the opposite extreme of over-informality may water down the concentration until the worship fails to perform its representative function and the sense of concerted action by the Church corporately is dissipated.

In view of this integral connexion between the whole of life and, within it, specific times and objects with which we associate deliberate, articulate worship, it is interesting to find what later became technical terms of worship (and some of them were already beginning to carry such associations) employed in the New Testament to describe the dedicated activity of entire Christian lives. Thus, addressing the Christians in Rome, St. Paul describes it as God's gracious gift to him

[1] "Kult im antiken Sinn gibt es nicht mehr in der neutestamentlichen Gemeinde" —*Gemeinde und Gemeindeordnung im Neuen Testament*, 1959, 201.

INDEX

REPRINT OF A CLASSIC

Worship in the New Testament by C. F. D. Moule, originally published by Lutterworth Press in 1961, has been out of print for over a decade. The continuing demand for the book has led to its being reprinted in the Grove Liturgical Study series in 1977-8 in two parts, but now as a double-size Study.

GROVE LITURGICAL STUDIES (32 or 40 pages—price **£1.50**). This series began in March 1975, and is published quarterly. Nos. 1-5 are out of print. The studies are designed to be weightier, whilst still within the range of interest for non-specialists and students. Asterisked numbers have been reprinted.

ISSN 0306–0608   **ISBN** 0 907536 52 2

GROVE BOOKS

BRAMCOTE NOTTS. NG9 3DS (0602-251114)

Printed by Hassall & Lucking Ltd, Cross Street, Long Eaton, Nottingham, NG10 1HD   Tel. L.E. 3292